D0591307

THE
BIG
BOOK OF
FOOTBALL'S
FUNNIEST
QUOTES

This edition published in 2009

Copyright © Carlton Books Limited 2009

Carlton Books Limited
20 Mortimer Street
London W1T 3JW

A CIP catalogue record for this book is available from the British Library

Includes materieal previously published in both *Pulled Off at Half-Time* by Stuart Reeves and *Playing in the Hole* by Adrian Clarke and Iain Spragg.

ISBN: 978-1-84732-379-8

The publishers would like to thank the following sources for their kind permission to reproduce the pictures in this book.

Every effort has been made to acknowledge correctly and contact the source and/or copyright holder of each picture and Carlton Books Limited apologises for any unintentional errors or omissions, which will be corrected in future editions of this book.

Printed in Great Britain

THE BIG BOOK OF FOOTBALL'S FUNNIEST QUOTES

CARLTON

CONTENTS

FOREWORD
By Peter Shilton OBE

Football without laughter just wouldn't be the same as there's always been a rich of vein of humour running throughout the game – fans joking with players, players with journalists, and, believe it or not, even players having a laugh with managers and referees!

Put any group of young lads together and there'll be a certain amount of high jinx and mickey-taking going on, but when it comes to a football team it would seem all the more apparent. This is largely due to the amount of time the team spends together – often training, eating and rooming together – and running jokes and jests are bound to develop over time. This joking not only helps the team get along but the laughter often relieves the pressure of any forthcoming fixture.

The Big Book of Football's Funniest Quotes is a fine collection of comical offerings courtesy of game's the players, managers, pundits and commentators. There are smart quips, barmy remarks and more than a few confused commentaries. Sure, a few of the players, managers and commentators might be a bit embarrassed by some of the daft things they've said – but we've all said similar things in our time – and the ability to laugh at yourself is all part of the spirit and camaraderie of the dressing room.

Peter Shilton

Legendary goalkeeper Peter Shilton holds the record for playing more professional games than any other player (1005). His international career, spanning 20 years, earned him 125 caps, making him England's most capped player.

INTRODUCTION

As the old saying goes, footballers like to let their feet do the talking, and judging by this brand spanking new collection of metaphor-mangling, tongue-twisting verbal volleys, it's an adage they should certainly stick to.

Let's face facts, those associated with the beautiful game aren't exactly renowned for their eloquence. Even the professionals behind the microphone are prone to the curse of "foot-in-mouth" disease that seems to strike down the great and the good, and with virtually every new interview, post-match press conference and tirade, a classic clanger is added to the collection.

The great Tottenham Hotspur manager Bill Nicholson once had this to say on the subject of intelligence in footballers:

"Intelligence doesn't make you a good footballer. Oxford and Cambridge would have the best sides if that were true. It's a football brain that matters and that doesn't usually go with an academic brain. I prefer players not to be too good or too clever at other things. It means they concentrate on football."

Now there are certainly plenty of examples to back this up but it could also be applied to managers, commentators and pundits alike. Often though, football people come up with the smartest quips, wisecracks and one-liners that any academic or poet laureate would be proud of, and that – along with the usual mixed-metaphors, general confusion, mangling of language and post-match interview cliches – is what *The Big Book of Football's Funniest Quotes* is all about!

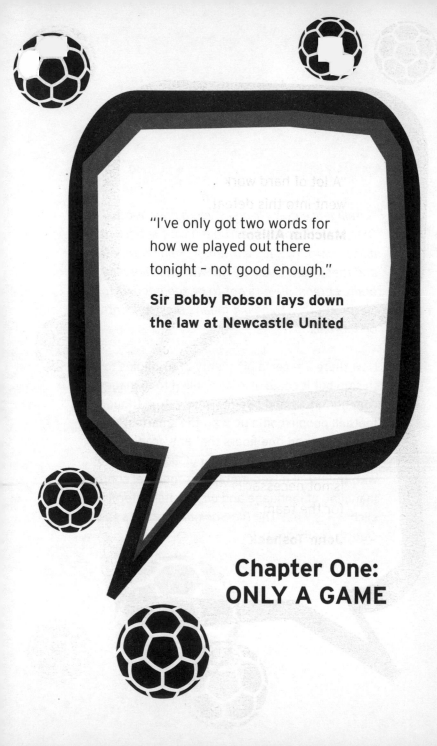

"I've only got two words for how we played out there tonight - not good enough."

Sir Bobby Robson lays down the law at Newcastle United

Chapter One:
ONLY A GAME

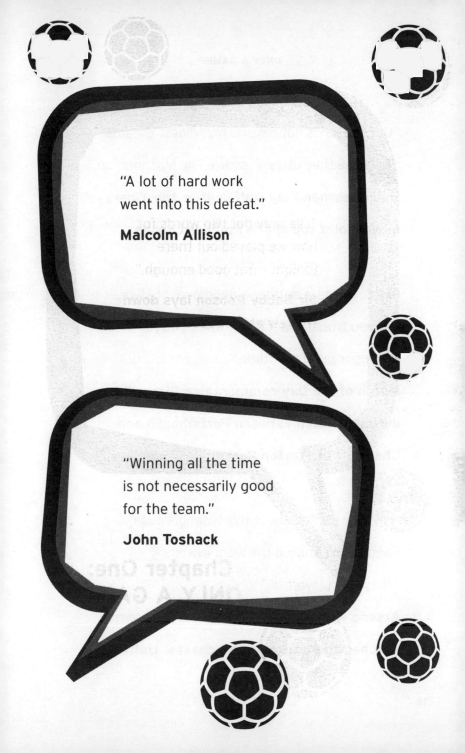

"Our season is not beyond my wildest dreams

- because they usually involve Elle Macpherson."

Hull chairman Paul Duffen after the Tigers

moved joint top of the Premier League

"Ashley Cole is getting a good deal of stick,

but you would expect that when you're

playing away from home."

Match of the Day commentator Steve Wilson

during a match between Portsmouth and

Chelsea - at Fratton Park.

"I'm very excited about this team because

- and I don't know if the word exists

- they are 'playerish'."

Arsene Wenger on his Arsenal team have

watched them take on Manchester United

"Kenny Dalglish came on at the same time as me and everyone expected him to win it for Liverpool. But here I was, a ginger-haired nobody, setting up the winning goal for Arsenal."
Perry Groves on the 1987 League Cup final win over Liverpool

"We're in football to play in big games. And games don't come any bigger than the semi-final of the Cup at Hampden."
John Collins doesn't rate Hibs' chances of making the final

"I would not be bothered if we lost every game as long as we won the league."
Mark Viduka

"Training was terribly slack. Players strolled up at any old time. Some would just walk round the track and one used to go over the far side for a smoke"

Peter McParland, scorer in the 1957 FA Cup Final, describes life at Aston Villa in the 1950s.

"I thought it was a bit high – he nearly took my willy off. You would probably expect that from Bob but there you go."

Inverness' Ross Tokely is a forgiving soul

"I should have punched him harder."

Eric Cantona on the infamous kung-fu incident at Selhurst Park

"It got to the point where I just thought, 'I'm going to take everyone on.' And when I got through I just hit it as hard as I could. David Seaman got a lot of stick, but it really was the only place I could have put it to beat him."

Ryan Giggs describing his wonder goal in the 1999 FA Cup semi-final replay against Arsenal

"Ryan just put his head down, ran like he always does, didn't pass and got lucky."

Nicky Butt's view of Giggs' goal

"We lost because we didn't win."

Ronaldo

"If you don't believe you can win, there is no point in getting out of bed at the end of the day."
Neville Southall

"If we win, we go to the semi-final. If we lose, I will go to Earl's Court and watch the wrestling on the 24th."
Jose Mourinho has his bases covered ahead of Chelsea's Champions League quarter-final

"It's great to get the first trophy under the bag."
Michael Owen

"The familiar sight of Liverpool lifting the League Cup for the first time..."
Barry Davies

"That will always be a memory for everyone
else I suppose. The winner's medal and scoring
the goal are my memories."
**Steve Morrow reflects on being dropped by
Tony Adams and breaking his collar bone
after the 1993 League Cup final replay**

"Before we won the Championship,
I told the lads exactly how many goals
we would score and how many points.
I was exactly right. I'm brilliant!"
**Manchester City manager Malcolm
Allison in 1972**

"Well, we got nine and you can't score more than that."

Sir Bobby Robson on a 9-0 thrashing of Luxembourg in 1960, in which he played

"After 15 years, I'm an overnight success."

José Mourinho

"The world looks a totally different place after two wins. I can even enjoy watching Blind Date or laugh at Noel's House Party."

Gordon Strachan is clearly losing his marbles

"There's no in-between - you're either good or bad. We were in between."

Gary Lineker

"I played my way into the side when I had a good training session the day before the derby match. I kicked a few of the lads and the manager saw that"

Middlesborough's Lee Cattermole, then 17, describes how he earned his debut at Newcastle

"Newcastle had not won in 29 games and two plus nine is 11. While they were scoring the winning goals, I was running round the outside of the ground 11 times to lift the hoodoo. I arrived late and had no ticket. But the moment I got out of the car and touched the Highbury stadium, Ray Parlour was sent off."

Uri Geller inspires a Newcastle victory that ended a 30-game winless run in London

"People said that I must have kept all the bricks that came through my window and put a snooker room on the side of my house. I did keep the bricks but I built a five-bedroom detached house in Wilmslow with them."

Steve Daley, 1979 British transfer record-holder, after life at Manchester City turned sour

"This is not a reality check for us because we never thought we were Brazil."

Christian Dailly reflects on Scotland's defeat to Belarus

"Winning all the time is not necessarily good for the team."

John Toshack

"If you can manage Celtic, you can be Prime Minister."

Gordon Strachan has political ambitions

"I'm not disappointed - just disappointed."

Kevin Keegan

"Not many people can say they scored at the Bernabéu so I was quite pleased, although I don't know how happy [goalkeeper] Bobby Mimms was."

Alan Harper on his own goal in a 1987 Everton friendly with Real Madrid

"A lot of hard work went into this defeat."

Malcolm Allison

"We're football people, not poets, but obviously I'm disappointed with the result."

Mick McCarthy definitely not a poet

"We must have had 99 per cent of the game. It was the other 3 per cent that cost us the match."

Ruud Gullit

"This is not a reality check for us because we never thought we were Brazil."

Christian Dailly

"Up front we played like world beaters – at the back it was more like panel beaters."

Paul Jewell

"If you never concede a goal you're going to win more games than you lose."
Bobby Moore

"If I didn't have a will to win or it didn't hurt anymore when I got beaten, I would have retired years ago."
Manchester City manager Stuart Pearce responds to being asked if a 4-0 defeat at West Bromwich Albion hurt

"I don't believe in superstitions. I just do certain things because I'm scared in case something will happen if I don't do them."
Michael Owen fails to grasp the whole "superstitious" concept

"I'm looking for a goalkeeper with three legs."

Sir Bobby Robson after Shay Given is

nutmegged twice by Marcus Bent of

Ipswich Town

"We have all had more fun than this.

Have you ever known a colder night?"

Martin Keown after the defeat by Shakhtar

Donetsk in Moscow, November 2000

"That's the way I am and I always will be.

After all, I kick Laurent Robert in training

– and he's one of our players."

Newcastle United's Andy Griffin on his

no-nonsense training philosophy

"We lost because we didn't win."

Brazil's Ronaldo

"England were beaten in the sense

that they lost."

Dickie Davis

"When you score goals you are great.

When you don't you are fat."

Ronaldo, definitely isn't bitter

"Everything's been really positive and smooth.

Apart from, obviously, the season."

**David Beckham is determined to remain

positive after signing for LA Galaxy**

"I would have given my right arm to be a pianist."

Bobby Robson

"He's like a second wife."

Benni McCarthy on his relationship with strike partner Jason Roberts

"I can see where the referee was getting confused – he does look like so many of my players."

Steve Coppell on the sending off of club mascot Kingsley the lion – his Reading team kit was confusing the officials.

"I just felt that the whole night, the conditions and taking everything into consideration and everything being equal, and everything is equal, we should have got something from the game – but we didn't."
John Barnes with some classic football-speak

"I feel OK. The only difference is in training you have the press – and they want to come home and sleep with you."
Thierry Henry enjoys an intimate relationship with the Spanish media

"Two questions - why were England so poor, and if they were poor, why?"

Commentator Ian Payne

"England had no direction but more formations than a ballroom-dancing team."

Terry Butcher, unimpressed by England's defeat in Northern Ireland in 2005

"Their keeper played very well and it was not the best pitch, but I am not making excuses."

Graham Rix

"We didn't have the run of the mill."

Glenn Hoddle

"We pressed the self-destruct button ourselves."
Brian Kidd

"We mustn't be despondent. We don't have to play them every week - although we do play them next week as it happens."
Sir Bobby Robson after a 2-0 league defeat to Arsenal who Newcastle United were to face a week later in the FA Cup

"We climbed three mountains and then proceeded to throw ourselves off them."
Billy McNeill, Celtic manager, after winning 5-4 in a topsy-turvy European Cup-Winners' Cup tie with Partizan Belgrade, but going out on away goals on an aggregate 6-6 score in 1989

"The circus came to town but the lions and tigers didn't turn up."
Newcastle United's Kevin Keegan after losing at Old Trafford in December 1995

"I've only got two words for how we played out there tonight – not good enough."
Sir Bobby Robson lays down the law at Newcastle United

"It was very nice to enter the locker room. There was a good feeling in there, and I got a good feeling from Kevin Doyle and Stephen Hunt."
Reading new boy Marek Matejovsky is touched by his special welcome

"To get players to come to Plymouth I had to beat them up and drug them."
Ian Holloway's drastic method to recruit new players

"Our major problem is that we don't know how to play football."
Sam Allardyce

"I have always tried to look at the positive, even when you are in 10 miles of traffic on the M25."
Alan Pardew

"If they hadn't scored, we would've won."
Howard Wilkinson

"I said I wanted the same car as James Bond and the reporter got the wrong end of the stick and said I wanted to be James Bond."
Joe Cole

"That's a home win and an away draw inside four days. We've only got one more game in November, and if we win that, I'm in grave danger of becoming Manager of the Month."
Mike Walker, four days before he was sacked in November 1994

"Chelsea has Roman Abramovich and his millions made from Russian oilfields and we've got Barry Hearn who does own a rather lucrative snooker hall in Ilford.
Comedian and Leyton Orient fan Bob Mills

"We nearly did not sign him because the letters did not fit on his shirt."

Arsenal's David Dein on the signing of Giovanni van Bronckhorst

"Our prices are half Newcastle's prices – you just can't compare the clubs, they're not to compare. We're stuck between a massive city that's vibrant like Newcastle... and Middlesbrough."

Sunderland chairman Bob Murray

"We know we have to score goals, be strong in defence and kill teams in the first half."

William Gallas is nothing if not aggressive

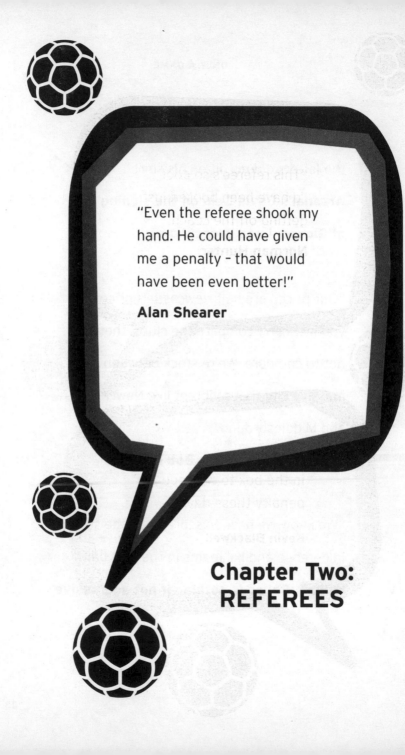

"Even the referee shook my hand. He could have given me a penalty – that would have been even better!"

Alan Shearer

Chapter Two: REFEREES

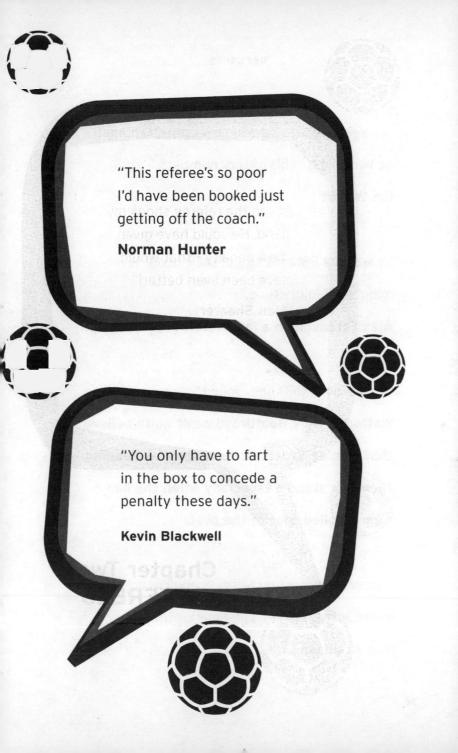

"The referee was booking everyone. I thought he was filling in his lottery numbers."
Ian Wright

"It was the 95th minute of their usual seven minutes of injury time."
Alex Ferguson on a late Aston Villa equaliser

"It was like a UFO had landed."
Watford's Aidy Boothroyd can't quite believe that referee Stuart Atwell allowed a Reading "goal" to stand - especially when the ball clearly rolled wide of the post.

"I never comment on referees and I'm not going to break the habit of a lifetime for that prat."
Ron Atkinson

"As for the fourth official, he is a doughnut."

Gary Megson

"I didn't know you were a Spurs fan."

Blackburn Rovers boss Graeme Souness

to referee Graham Poll during the game at

Ewood Park with Tottenham Hotspur in 2003

"I don't know about making referees

professional. They love themselves

enough as it is now."

Paul Scholes

"We asked the fourth official to tell the referee to stop the game and take away the balloons – or kill them."

Sven-Goran Eriksson after a bunch of balloons threatened to derail his Manchester City side's FA Cup run at Sheffield United.

"You know me – I always listen to referees."

Roy Keane – just after receiving notice of an FA disciplinary charge

"This referee's so poor I'd have been booked just getting off the coach."

Norman Hunter watching Mike Reed in 1998

"The referee in question was not one of my favourite people. In fact anyone who cr*ps in Graham Poll's toilet can't be all bad."

Referee Jeff Winter on the Robbie Savage toilet incident

"I can't take responsibility for the referee handing out bookings if people breathe too heavily."

Joe Royle

"Don't talk about the game, talk about Uriah Rennie - that's what he likes and he's always been the same."

Kevin Keegan on his favourite referee

"I personally think referees should be wired up to a couple of electrodes and they should be allowed to make three mistakes before you run 50,000 volts through their genitals."

John Gregory

"The referee made three mistakes only. The red card, playing too much time at the end of the first half and the penalty. Apart from that he was good."

Avram Grant isn't one to criticise officials

"The problem with officials is that sometimes they get too officious."

There's just no pleasing Andy Gray

"We'll see you in the second half for the next
part of the Uriah Rennie show."
**Preston's half-time announcer isn't
impressed with Mr Rennie**

"We were robbed. That is the second time this
season that referee has ruined a game for me.
He spoilt the night. I am almost speechless."
George Boateng, not quite speechless

"The officials were the worst team tonight.
They were indecisive throughout and there was
practically manslaughter on James Scowcroft."
Neil Warnock loses his sense of perspective

"Referees aren't looking at what they should be looking at. You need to prioritise. It seems the main issue this season is whether three or four Chelsea players surround referees, or say things they shouldn't say."

Avram Grant feels the pressure

"We asked the fourth official to tell the referee to stop the game and take away the balloons – or kill them."

Sven-Goran Eriksson really hates parties

"You only have to fart in the box to concede a penalty these days."

Kevin Blackwell smells a conspiracy

"Those decisions cost us three points and possibly £50m. Dowd by name, Dowd by nature. The only thing consistent about these fellas is their inconsistency."

Paul Jewell won't be sending Phil Dowd a Christmas card this year

"Because you're Australian and you always beat us at everything."

David Elleray explains his decision to book an Australian player

"Once apon a time, if you told people you were from Tring they'd say 'Oh yeah, that's where Walter Rothschild is from'. Now they say 'That's where that bloody referee lives."

Graham Poll puts Tring on the map

"I know Rob Styles. He will get up in the morning, look in the mirror and wonder how the other seven wonders of the world got on."

Ray Houghton reckons referees are getting vainer

"Some referees don't like it. They don't like the truth. But I just told him how bad he was in the first half."

Sir Alex Ferguson exchanges pleasantries with Mark Clattenburg

"If the referee stands by that decision, I have two wooden legs. I won't be seeing this ref again in my dreams – and I won't be kissing him!"

Ian Holloway

He gave the penalty and then he pointed the
other way. It's a disgrace. I don't know
 what he sent me off for – I wasn't listening.
Walking on the pitch perhaps?"
Dennis Wise is distinctly unimpressed

"I've got to be very careful with that I say about
the referee because I thought he was poor all
game really."
**Middlesbrough's Luke Young fails to
hold his tongue**

"It is difficult to lose the game on a wrong decision. It was offside and it is proven on TV. Why do we have to take it? I still don't think it's right. We have to do something about it. Yes, I am angry."

Arsene Wenger is definitely not happy

"The referee was punching the air when they scored."

Neil Warnock as his Crystal Palace side concede a late equaliser

"Thank heavens the official is an intimate friend of mine. I talk with the referee all the time. We speak together regularly and, when we are able, we dine together."

Barcelona boss Frank Rijkaard teases Chelsea rival Jose Mourinho

"They call themselves professional. They're not professional. Professional means you're good."

Paul Jewell, a fan of amateur officials

"It was like the ref had a brand new yellow card and wanted to see if it worked."

Richard Rufus

"We've got a Mickey Mouse ref doing nothing."

Joe Kinnear

"It not only looked a soft penalty – it was a soft penalty"

Adam Miller, Gillingham skipper gives his verdict on a penalty award.

"We had Phil Dowd at Arsenal last year and we were denied three stonewall penalties so maybe he has it in his Premier League contract that he doesn't give away penalties against Arsenal."

Paul Jewell expands on a theme

"Are the rules you can go first for the man when the ball is in the air and everybody decides it's not a foul, or do we make it a judo party and maybe everybody will be happy?"

Arsene Wenger again, still not satisfied

"Even the referee shook my hand. He could have given me a penalty - that would have been even better!"
Alan Shearer is a hard man to please

"It's almost impossible for referees these days - they need eyes in the back of their heads which they haven't got."
Graham Taylor took biology GCSE

"I think they just want the referee to blow up at this point."
Martin O'Neill sums up everyone's feelings

"I was surprised first of all that I was sent off for what I said. It's like if the speed limit is 60mph – sometimes you are not caught when you drive 70mph and sometimes you are caught when you drive 61mph. I drove 60.5mph."

Arsene Wenger is banished to the stands

"Newcastle are a good team, like Everton. At Everton, there are 30,000 referees, in Newcastle there are 50,000."

Jose Mourinho sees referees everywhere

"The referee has a reputation for trying to make a name for himself."

Graeme Souness

"I don't know if the referee was wearing a Barcelona shirt because they kicked me all over the place. If the referee did not want us to win, he should have said so from the off."
Thierry Henry suspects favouritism

"Rooney was complaining all the time, protests and more protests. He reminded me of my kids."
World Cup official Horacio Elizondo

"We had a referee who, in my opinion, wasn't up to the required standard and that isn't bleating about the referee."
Burnley boss Steve Cotterill is definitely, absolutely not complaining

"As for the fourth official, he is a doughnut."

And Bolton boss Gary Megson reckons the referee is a Danish pastry

"Mark Halsey didn't have a decision to make, apart from giving the penalty."

Chris Kamara can't quite make his mind up

"I just think the FA are inherently weak when it comes to these issues. We've been eroding the power of the referee for years and years. I've been refereeing in the Premiership since 1993, I'm the most experienced referee they've got and yet my credibility no longer holds."

Graham Poll lets rip

"McCarthy shakes his head in agreement
with the referee."
Martin Tyler is no body language expert

"I know referees have a difficult job to do
and he's not helped by the antics of a striker
who's thrown himself around for most of
the match. He was on the floor more
than he was standing up."
**A rare moment of empathy for officials
from Steve Bruce**

"If the referee stands by that decision, I have
two wooden legs. I will be seeing this ref again
in my dreams - and I won't be kissing him."
**Ian Holloway has nightmares about the
match officials**

"I thought Michael Johnson should have had a penalty but the referee booked him for filming."

Sven-Goran Eriksson should have told his players to leave their camcorders in the dressing room

"Rafa is trying to get the referee on his side. He must think we are bloody stupid."

Sir Alex Ferguson wants referee Steve Bennett all too himself

Cristiano. Why would he want to go down? He was on a hat-trick, he had gone round the keeper and he was brought down. It was a ridiculous decision."

Sir Alex Ferguson is outraged

"The official has got his hand on Joe Jordan's backside."
Commentator Alan Green exposes the seedy side of match day refereeing

"We had two different referees. In the first half he was laid back and let things go. In the second half he was a terror."
Steve Coppell reckons Mark Clattenburg is football's answer to Jekyll and Hyde

"I could have another moan but I'm sick to death of my own whingeing."

Steve Bruce

Chapter Three: MANAGERS

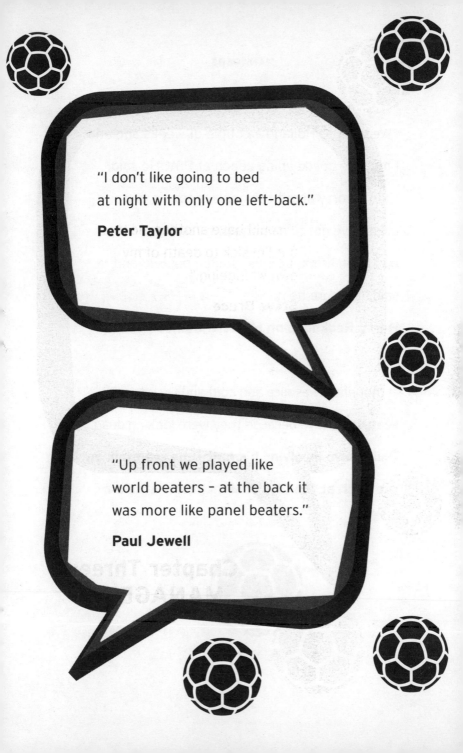

"We went to Holland a couple of weeks ago and I met the goalkeeping coach at PSV. He said, 'Don't worry about the goalkeeper, he is world class'. I've got to be honest, I wasn't sure if he had been drinking. I just smiled politely and said, 'I'm sure he is'.

Harry Redknapp on Heulero Gomes

"I thought it was nice and cold and I wanted to keep them alive because they were looking dead."

Phil Brown on giving his half-time teamtalk on the pitch at the City of Manchester stadium

"On a great day in American electoral history, I would like to remind him of Abraham Lincoln's great quotation - 'You can fool some of the people all of the time. But you cannot fool all of the people all of the time."

Stoke's Tony Pulis gets topical in response to Arsene Wenger's accusation that his side were thugs after his team's 1-0 victory.

"In the supermarket you have class one, two or class three eggs and some are more expensive than others and some give you better omelettes. So when the class one eggs are in Waitrose and you cannot go there, you have a problem."

Apparently Jose Mourinho would never shop in Tesco

"I've learned that you have to score goals
to win games."

Rafa Benitez is nothing if not a tactical genius

"I think I must have run over six black cats
since I've been at Wolves."

**The RSPCA wants a word with Wolves
boss Glenn Hoddle**

"We've had the snow this week, so we've done
very little training. We've built an igloo and had
a snowball fight, so we might have to put the
balls away in future and take the players to a
snowdome instead."

**Aidy Boothroyd reveals Watford's
revolutionary training techniques**

"Up front we played like world beaters - at the back it was more like panel beaters."

Paul Jewell doesn't rate the Wigan defence then

"Their goals were just comedy. You'd probably win £250 on Candid Camera for that second one."

Crystal Palace boss Neil Warnock's verdict on his side's defending

"The good thing about these early kick-offs is that you can go out for a meal and still be all in your pyjamas for half eight."

Neil Warnock likes his early nights

"Ricardo has worked with me for four years and I do not understand these quotes, he probably needs to see a doctor."

Jose Mourinho wants a word with Ricardo Carvalho

"Once Ashley [Young] puts some weight on he will be fantastic. At the moment he's about three-and-a-half stone – a couple of times we have put him through the letterbox."

Martin O'Neill likes to post his players

"You talk about Ronaldo and Messi. Is Young in that company? Yes. I've just put him in it."

Martin O'Neill is very happy with Ashley Young's weight now

"The reception I got at Upton Park wasn't too bad considering I now manage one of their biggest rivals. Mind you, it helped that I didn't get out of my seat for ninety minutes."

Harry Redknapp now of Spurs

"It's up to the fans to help me now. If they see any member of my squad in a pub, club, bar, whatever, I want them to ring me up and tell me. If my players want to drink they can get pissed in the safety of their own homes."

Neil Warnock favours a tipple indoors

"It's like having a blanket that is too small for the bed. You pull the blanket up to keep your chest warm and your feet stick out. I cannot buy a bigger blanket because the supermarket is closed. But the blanket is made of cashmere."
Jose Mourinho stretches his supermarket analogy to breaking point

"Today's game is a 30-pointer."
Billy Davies gets a little carried away

"The match for them is a bit like people down south going to the theatre. They want to be entertained."
Kevin Keegan highlights the great north-south divide

"He really is special. If he runs at you, you're in trouble. He'll do 14 stepovers and give you twisted blood."

Harry Redknapp on Cristiano Ronaldo

"We went for a walk before the game and a bird dumped right on my head. They say that can be a lucky omen - and it was!"

Barnsley boss Simon Davey after his side knocked Liverpool out of the FA Cup

"If you want to sleep, you don't become a football manager."

Steve Coppell suffers from insomnia

"We develop players. We don't have them growing in greenhouses out the back because we don't have time for greenhouses. We're more of a microwave sort of club."

Aidy Boothroyd wants quick results

"I'm not an electrician, even though I'm known as 'Sparky'. But I was hoping the lights would stay off."

Mark Hughes welcomes a floodlight failure at Upton Park

"I couldn't be more chuffed if I were a badger at the start of the mating season."

Ian Holloway – student of amorous animals

"I don't like going to bed at night

with only one left-back."

Peter Taylor on problems with

personnel at Wycombe

"The only way we will be getting to Europe

is on Easyjet in the summertime!"

Steve Coppell plays down expectations

"If I were a fisherman, I would never think

I'm not going to catch a single fish."

Gerard Houllier is an optimistic angler

"I know what is around the corner

- I just don't know where the corner is."

The genius of Kevin Keegan

"Our programme didn't do us any favours. We've been handicapped by the Premier League in the fixture list. They tell me it's not planned. Bloody hell!"

Sir Alex Ferguson questions the fixture list

"You could never tell what these people are doing. Even if I was sitting having breakfast with them I would not know what they were thinking."

Sir Alex Ferguson again, this time on the FA's decision to ban Patrice Evra for four matches after his confrontation with a Chelsea groundsman at Stamford Bridge.

"Manchester United defended with great spirit and a lot of effort and their future is only looking better for them now. But they are not good enough to be champions, only to finish closer to us and not drop quite so many points."
Jose Mourinho heaps faint praise on United

"He has that smell to be where he needs to be at the decisive moment. When there is chocolate to take in the box, he is there."
Arsene Wenger reckons Julio Baptista knows a thing or two about Quality Street

"Was it as good as sex? Probably, yeah.
It's a long while since I've had sex – you'd
have to ask the wife."
**Iain Dowie reveals a little too much after
Coventry snatch a late equaliser**

"I was excited and it takes a lot to get me
excited... ask my wife!"
...As does Roy Keane

"It wasn't a monkey on my back,
it was Planet of the Apes!"
Mick McCarthy's classic primate pun

"I banned the players from stuffing their faces with chocolate. On the bus, the players chanted 'we want our chocolate bars'."

Arsene Wenger could have a riot on his hands

"I cannot put into words just how much promotion means to me but if I could I would put it in a can so I could open it later."

Reading boss Steve Coppell feels like celebrating promotion with a few cans

"The challenge on Robbie Savage has been brushed under the table."

There must a shortage of carpets chez Mark Hughes

"I told them they were the best players in the country, so to go and play like it. When they left the dressing room, I expected a response."

Sir Alex Ferguson on the half-time teamtalk which saw Manchester United overturn a 3-0 deficit at the break and beat Spurs 5-3

"Hopefully we can go to Arsenal and keep a clean sheet. But it will be very difficult. Anything can happen at Highbury. Maybe hundreds of squirrels will come on to the pitch and we will have a problem. You cannot prepare for things like that. We will probably have to run from them."

Martin Jol is preparing for anything ahead of the north London derby

"He wears a suit, so he's a tactician. He wears a tracksuit, so he's a motivator. He carries a clipboard, so he's a bus conductor."
Stuart Pearce on the many talents of Rafa Benitez

"I've got too many Cavaliers in my side and not enough Roundheads. Too many players with plumes and feathers but not enough hard workers. And the Roundheads won in the end."
Paul Sturrock loves his history

"I know I asked for patience
- but not that much!"
Sven-Goran Eriksson after England's last-gasp 2-2 draw against Greece which secured qualification for the 2006 World Cup

"Is he entitled to go dance with his wife at a do? Yes he is. Does he need some help with his dance moves? Obviously he does. We will do some more movement to music in training."
Palace boss Iain Dowie leaps to Andrew Johnson's defence

"It just came in so quickly, he tried to get a head on it but it came off the wrong corner of his head."
Nigel Worthington has too many square-headed players

"I would love to say the goal was well rehearsed on the training ground, but we've not been there for three weeks because it has been flooded."
Steve Bruce is nothing if not honest

"I could have another moan but I'm sick to death of my own whingeing."
Steve Bruce decides to keep quiet

"It was awful. Sometimes you have one or two players who are not doing their job, but on this occasion we had about a dozen."
Maths was never Sven-Goran Eriksson's strong point

"I watched Arsenal in the Champions League the other week, playing some of the best football I've ever seen, and yet they couldn't have scored in a brothel with two grand in their pockets."

Ian Holloway reckons the Gunners are firing blanks

"Apparently he was eating a lasagne and somehow pulled a hamstring - it has to be a world first."

Micky Adams is mystified by his injury list

"It's a bit strange if you're a player to see remarks on the TV but there's no problem with Jermain. After the story, I told him I wouldn't swap him for Miss World – he would probably swap me for Miss World though."

Martin Jol fancies Jermain Defoe

"My family are really happy here at Liverpool and I am prepared to have my daughter with a Scouse accent, even though it is sometimes a problem for me."

Rafa Benitez is prepared to make big sacrifices to stay on Merseyside

"When I hear them say they can win the title it makes me feel like laughing."

Jose Mourinho doesn't rate Liverpool's title chances then

"We are like the primary school boys walking into the secondary school for the first time and finding out who the bully boys are."

Derby boss Billy Davies rolls with the blows after promotion to the Premier League

"Sadly, I have been unable to persuade FIFA, UEFA and the Premier League to allow me to use 12 players in every game."

Rafa Benitez thinks Liverpool deserve special favours

"If it was a boxing match, it would be Muhammad Ali against Jimmy Krankie."
Fight fan Aidy Boothroyd reflects on Watford's defeat to Manchester United

"We know it's going to be very difficult because Mark McGhee and Scott Leitch are winners. They showed that last year by finishing third."
Aberdeen boss Jimmy Calderwood damns Motherwell's coaching staff with faint praise

"When you are in a dogfight, you have to fight like dogs. If it is a gunfight, you can't afford to go in with just a knife."
Chris Coleman fancies a fight

"I said to my wife, 'come on, it's Valentine's Night, I will take you out somewhere special'. So I took her to Brentford against Southend."
Alan Curbishley is an old romantic really

"They have my credit card number and we will say, 'How much do you need this week? Let's do it.'"
Arsene Wenger loves his trips to face the FA's disciplinary panel

"It was a terrific game, but I'd rather it had been a load of crap and we'd won."
Harry Redknapp doesn't pull his punches

"We went to watch a Billy Joel show. Half of the foreign lads weren't quite sure who Billy Joel was, but I enjoyed it anyway. For the Charlton game I'll really punish them – I'll take them to see Mamma Mia."

It's tough playing for Harry Redknapp...

"Young players are a little bit like melons. Only when you open and taste the melon are you 100% sure that the melon is good. Sometimes you have beautiful melons, but they don't taste very good and some other melons are a bit ugly and when you open them, the taste is fantastic."

Jose Mourinho gets fruity

"You can compare us at the moment to a bit of soft porn – there is an awful lot of foreplay and not a lot going on in the box."

Rochdale manager Keith Hill wants more "action"

"I don't read the papers, I don't gamble, I don't even know what day it is!"

Steve McClaren confirms what we all suspected

"Seriously, the boy glides across the park. If he walked across a puddle, he wouldn't make a splash."

Harry Redknapp thinks Theo Walcott is the Messiah

"This transfer window should not be allowed. Us managers can only buy all our shopping in four weeks and just imagine if that was the case for Christmas shopping. You can imagine the queues."

Maybe Ian Holloway should buy new players online

"In all my time as a manager, I've never met a team that is unbeatable."

Sven-Goran Eriksson tries to look on bright side as England are drawn in the 2006 World Cup's so-called Group of Death.

"He reminds me of a hunting dog. When I want something specific done, he is very willing to learn."

Rafa Benitez sings Jamie Carragher's canine praises

"Steven Gerrard had his house burgled last week but we were robbed in broad daylight here."

Brian Laws shows his sympathetic side after Sheffield Wednesday lose to Palace

"All the restaurants were full and we couldn't get in, so we celebrated with a takeaway kebab instead."

Neil Warnock treats his players to a doner and chips

"If we win, we go to the semi-final. If we lose, I will go to Earls Court and watch the wrestling on the 24th with my children."
Jose Mourinho plans ahead

"He had so much space you could have put a bungalow in there for his retirement."
Mick McCarthy wants the Wolves defence to tighten up

"I have seen the film The Alamo and right now I feel like I've got Davy Crockett behind me. Sometimes I feel like I could put my head in a bucket of water."
Stuart Pearce needs to cool down

"We were pumping in crosses when we should have been cuddling the ball."
Tactile tactics from Alan Curbishley

"It's a long time since I've seen a player who you feel would kick his granny to win, and that's lovely - though not for the granny."
Glenn Roeder has bad news for Steven Taylor's family

"For me it's been a good season, but we've only made a cake. Now we need to put the cherry on top."
Next season Rafa Benitez will buy the candles

"It's like a marriage. You want to do things in life but if you don't have anyone to share it with, then it's not as fulfilling."

Gareth Southgate sends an SOS to Middlesbrough's AWOL fans

"If we are going to go Americanized, we are going to have all these girls waving things every time there is a goal. You ask them to run up and down in Sheffield with very little clothing on - it would be hard work for them."

Neil Warnock isn't keen on unnecessary razzmatazz

"Look at my haircut. I am ready for the war."

Jose Mourinho idolised Action Man as a kid

"Despite the global warming, England is still not warm enough for him."
Arsene Wenger bids a fondish farewell to Spaniard Jose Reyes

"If a haulage company wanted a new lorry and someone said in September you cannot have one until January, it would not be allowed."
Gary Megson is worried about truck supplies

"I think we won that game against Liverpool because we scored and they didn't."
Nothing gets past Jose Mourinho

"People said I was pitting my wits against Sir Alex Ferguson but it is like using a water pistol to take on a machine gun."
Steve Bruce on Birmingham's defeat at Old Trafford

"I know the odd indulgence doesn't hurt players from time to time... besides, what can you do? Can you follow a player home to check if his missus is giving him steak and kidney pie for tea instead of pasta."
Harry Redknapp comes from the Old School

"If you can't pass a ball properly, a bowl of pasta's not going to make that much difference."

Redknapp's suspicious of the merits of football's dietary revolution

"We've got sports scientists who insist it's important for the lads to eat after games to refuel, even if it's 2am. I used to refuel after games at West Ham until half past three in the morning in a different way – but then I'm old school."

Redknapp reaffirms his credentials

"Football is all about winning, drawing and losing."

Peter Taylor covers the bases

"When you have an argument with your missus, you know when you're ready to go back and talk to her. You leave her alone for a bit because you know if you talk to her she will bite your head off. That's what life's about – and it's the same with footballers."

Tony Mowbray on his West Brom squad

"Not only have they taken my arms and legs, now they've cut my balls off."

Dennis Wise can't believe the FA after they docked Leeds 15 points

"That was like a Bond film where the villain has so many chances to kill him off, doesn't take them and eventually he comes back to bite them."

Lawrie Sanchez prefers a clean kill

"I had problems at first, confusing 'wine' and 'win' and my players would laugh."

Rafa Benitez has his Liverpool squad in stitches

"If they are naive and pure, then I'm Little Red Riding Hood."

Rafa Benitez isn't fooled by Arsenal

"Jens changed his mind but wasn't quick enough to respond to his brain."
Arsene Wenger on Jens Lehmann's two heads

"Mansfield gave us one hell of a game. I feared extra time but we are still on the march, still unbeaten, and I'm still a brilliant manager!"
Harry Redknapp loves himself

"At the moment we've only got 16 first-team players and my initials stand for Mick McCarthy, not Merlin the Magician."
McCarthy just can't conjure up any more bodies

"I'm not prone to outlandish predictions but this club can establish itself in the top eight of the Premier League."

Paul Jewell has big ambitions for Derby. Sort of.

"It was just handcuffs at dawn."

Alex Ferguson mixes his metaphors

"When we meet in airports we don't fight."

Apparently, Arsene Wenger likes to fight Alex Ferguson elsewhere

"I don't think we'll be professional for the full 90 minutes until the microchips are firmly imbedded in the players' heads."

Aidy Boothroyd has ground-breaking plans for his squad

"I was a young lad when I was growing up."

Nothing gets past David O'Leary

"It's about time us managers had a fight. I wouldn't be daft enough to have a go at Sam Allardyce but me and Bryan Robson would be decent. I'd have to kill him or he'd keep coming back at me!"

Steve Bruce has radical plans to liven up football

"At the moment, things are not going for us. We'd probably need a dog to run on the pitch to head it into the net for us."

Aidy Boothroyd isn't fussy where the goals come from

"Arsenal didn't have one single chance, including the goal."

Avram Grant and his rose-tinted spectacles

"Get hit in the bollocks, get hit in the nose, the gob, knock your crowns out. I'm not bothered but do not let it spin into the top corner."

Mick McCarthy favours physical defending

"I've just seen the replay again for the first time."

David Moyes is caught in a time loop

"When I was Walsall's manager, I didn't know you had to coach and train players."

Management came as a shock to Paul Merson

"It's just a game of football. There are 1.2 billion people in India who couldn't give a shit what happens to Reading."
You can't say Steve Coppell doesn't have a sense of perspective...

"I was never tempted to become a punk. I was Sidney Serious, I was into George Benson. I was smooth. Smooth as a cashmere codpiece."
Ian Holloway, anti-punk

"The best finishers are those strikers who don't care how many they miss."
Glenn Hoddle on the art of scoring goals

"Even the chef's been out for two weeks with a hernia."

Alan Curbishley laments West Ham's injury crisis

"I liked to ski-jump, but I couldn't out-jump Eddie The Eagle - he was special."

Sven-Goran Eriksson reveals his unusual sporting hero

"If we're not careful, we will be playing in high heels and skirts and playing netball."

Steve Bruce yearns for the days of football's true hardmen

"Emre has a left foot that can open a can of peas."
**Alex McLeish reckons the Turk is packing a
Swiss Army Knife**

"They searched the house and took a computer
away that I bought my wife two years ago – I
think she learnt to turn it on four weeks ago."
Harry Redknapp's missus needs IT advice

"People say we are having no luck,
but we are – it's just all bad."
**Gareth Southgate refuses to lose
his sense of humour**

"If you ask if I'd rather see Chelsea or Man
United win the title, then I will answer Arsenal."
Nul points for Arsene Wenger

"Some of our top players are out injured.

That's an excuse, but it's also not an excuse."

Wigan boss Chris Hutchings just can't

make his mind up

"The problem was conceding four goals

in the first half."

Rafa Benitez was happy with the

second 45 minutes

"My players travel more than Phileas Fogg

in Around The World In 80 Days. Javier

Mascherano had to play a friendly for

Argentina in Australia. That must have

been really important."

Rafa Benitez wants to keep the

Air Miles down

"By the time you read this we'll have had a scan on Fabregas. His foot blew up after the game and that's not the best sign."

Arsene Wenger on Fabregas's "explosive" foot

"I don't think my wife would be naked with anyone - she hardly ever gets naked with me. And with a face like mine, I don't blame her."

Ian Holloway knows he's no Brad Pitt

"I said it in pre-season. In fact, I may have said it before the season started."

Sir Alex Ferguson's logic: impeccable

"I'm pleased for Georgios [Samaras]. He can be a handful on any given day and trip over the ball on any given day."
Stuart Pearce offers distinctly qualified support for his player

"I saw Danny Mills and Robbie Savage lying next to each other, comparing tattoos - they seemed like lovers."
Paul Jewell reveals just how close his Derby players really are

"Kanu? He's about 47."
Harry Redknapp after 31-year-old Kanu scored to win the FA Cup for Portsmouth in 2008

"The crowd were dead. It was like a funeral out there."
Sir Alex Ferguson wants the Old Trafford faithful to liven up a bit

"I bought a Sade CD the other day and after listening to it for a while, I thought, 'Christ, no wonder she isn't famous any more'."
Ian Holloway, music critic

"He's just training here but we're well equipped to handle it. We have everything that's needed, including mirror doors."
Arsene Wenger can't wait for David Beckham to join the Gunners in training

"When we lost, I used to have so much trouble sleeping that I became addicted to Night Nurse. When I told my wife, she thought I was talking about some bird in suspenders."

Harry Redknapp on the medicinal wonders of cough medicine

"My confidence is 100 per cent in Frank Lampard but I told him if the next penalty is at a key point then it's better for another player to take the responsibility."

Jose Mourinho leaps to his player's defence

"It's the same if you told my wife I'm gay. A big laugh."

Martin Jol cracks himself up

"I'm not jumping on the Andy Johnson
for England bandwagon - I'm driving it."
Iain Dowie has his hands on the wheel

"The only way we will get into
Europe is by ferry."
**Kevin Keegan plans Newcastle's
team bonding trip**

"There was one point where I am sure
Richard Dunne thought he was Maradona."
**Sven-Goran Eriksson likes to brainwash
his players**

"People tell me he hasn't scored in open play for 11 months but he shouldn't force things. Maybe he has got to think about that a wee bit and then the chance will come. One might hit him on the backside and go in the net to start things off for him."
Alex McLeish bemoans Gary McSheffrey's bum deal

"I hated Robbie Savage when he played against me. He is one of those characters you despise when he is playing for the opposition, but you love when he is on your team."
Paul Jewell's love-hate relationship with the Wales midfielder

"I don't know if you know but with the
football kit today there are no pockets.
Nobody can put their hands in their pockets."

**Avram Grant has no idea where modern
players keep their spare change**

"Trust me, I'm comfortable not being
pals with people."

Roy "Cuddly" Keane

"I pinned the poem, 'If', by Rudyard Kipling,
up in the dressing room but I don't think
any of the players could make head or
tail of it. I left it up for an hour but took it
down before it got defaced."

Mike Newell thwarts Luton's graffiti artists

"I would love an Aston Martin but if you ask me £1 million for an Aston Martin, I tell you, you are crazy because they cost £250,000."
Jose Mourinho knows his motors

"The wife told me it looked as if I knew what I was doing a bit more."
Gareth Southgate trades in his tracksuit for a suit

"It looked like we'd picked 11 people off the streets and asked them if they fancied a game."
Steve Bruce isn't impressed

"Fail to prepare, prepare to fail."
Roy Keane, football poet

"It's no good having money in the bank and no good players out on the pitch."
Tony Mowbray is desperate to splash the cash

"Somebody's just given me a video of the game. I don't know why they handed it to me because there's no way I'm going to watch that again."
Neil Warnock won't torture himself any more

"Whenever a ball came towards them, it was like a bouncing bomb."
Steve Bruce witnesses an explosive encounter

"[Anthony] Stokes could be a top, top player in four or five years or he could be playing non-league."
Roy Keane hedges his bets

"If they don't want to come because their wife wants to go shopping in London, it's a sad state of affairs."
Roy Keane bemoans WAG power

"We were good friends until we started winning, then he started changing his mind."
Rafa Benitez falls out of love with Jose Mourinho

"I think the haircut helps. Having

my hair cut used to help me. I used

to feel leaner and sharper. Meaner.

So I might shave mine next month."

Roy Keane plans his next haircut

"The only feedback I've had off the chairman

is him asking me 'do you want a pie'?"

Steve Bruce settles in at Wigan

"I would love to gather all the fans

together to say goodbye but they

would crush me with their love."

Jose Mourinho's ego threatens

to get out of hand

"I've got more points on my licence
- I'm not joking!"
**Derby boss Paul Jewell on his side's
meagre points haul**

"Brian Clough kept my feet on the ground. Like
when he punched me after a game for making
a back pass."
Roy Keane relives the old days

"I've got to choose my words carefully but
I thought the supporters let us down badly
today. We needed them for the full 90
minutes today and we didn't get that.
And, for me, that's a disgrace."
**Norwich manager Peter Grant endears
himself to the crowd**

"I don't predict in football. All I predict is next week against Barnsley you will see a vastly different Norwich City team."
Glenn "I'm not Nostradamus" Roeder

"That's it with Owen - you shoot holes in him and he comes back for more."
Kevin Keegan, sharp shooter

"There are some guys who have this big telescope to look into the homes of other people and see what is happening. Wenger must be one of them and it is a sickness."
Jose Mourinho accuses the Arsenal manager of voyeurism

"Working with people on a field turns me on."

Graeme Souness has an outdoor fetish

"If you buy a man who is half-dead, everybody may be happy off the field, but on the field you'll have major problems."

Arsene Wenger likes his players alive and kicking

"I'm not going to make it a target, but it's something to aim for."

Steve Coppell has nothing in particular in his sights then

"You can play chess for about 10 hours and still lose, know what I mean?"

Sir Alex Ferguson, Grand Master

"The lad got over-excited when he saw the whites of the goalpost's eyes."
Steve Coppell gets over-excited in his post-match press conference

"The owner told me he wants to be in Europe within 18 months. Whether that means we're all going to Majorca next summer, I don't know."
Neil Warnock dusts off his passport

"I just thought 'sod it, let's just attack them'!"
Steve Coppell reveals his in-depth tactics

"I think there was just a little change today and I started to smell that things were improving a little bit."

David Moyes has a good nose for the game

"I'm not someone to fear things. They say in Holland 'have no fear, Jolly is here!'"
Martin Jol is scary back home

"Our major problem is that we don't know how to play football."
Sam Allardyce hits the nail on the head

"I've slept with a coat hanger in my mouth to keep the smile on my face these last couple of days."
Mick McCarthy has been having sleepless nights

"If I made a mistake then I
apologise. I am happy that I'm not
going to jail because of that."
Jose Mourinho doesn't want to do time

"He is flat out in the dressing room -
I just knocked him out. Now I might
go round and burn down his house."
**Wolves boss Dave Jones on his
"special" relationship with his former
player Chris Marsden**

"Intelligence doesn't make you a good footballer. Oxford and Cambridge would have the best sides if that were true. It's a football brain that matters and that doesn't usually go with an academic brain. I prefer players not to be too good or too clever at other things. It means they concentrate on football."

Bill Nicholson

"It was a surprise, but a very pleasant one. I had not planned to become a football club manager."

Arsenal physio Bertie Mee on being appointed Arsenal manager

"It's an incredible rise to stardom; at 17
you're more likely to get a call from Michael
Jackson than Sven-Göran Eriksson."
Gordon Strachan on Wayne Rooney

"If that lad makes a First Division footballer,
then I'm Mao Tse Tung."
**Tommy Docherty on Dwight Yorke after
his Aston Villa debut in 1990. Eight years
later he was sold to Manchester United for
£12.6 million**

"That's great, tell him he's Pelé and
get him back on."
**Partick Thistle manager, John Lambie,
when told a concussed striker did not
know who he was**

"The chairman of Brighton wouldn't recognize Gareth Barry if he was stood on Brighton beach in the team strip, with a seagull on his head and a ball in his hand."
Aston Villa manager John Gregory dismisses the claim that Brighton made Barry as a player

"I just wanted to give them some technical advice. I told them the game had started."
Ron Atkinson explaining why he moved from the stand to the dug-out during a game with Sheffield United in 1993

"What was my highlight of the tournament? Bumping into Frank Sinatra."
Ron Atkinson on the 1994 World Cup

"The only decisions I'm making at the moment are whether I have tea, coffee, toast or cornflakes in the morning."

Sam Allardyce after being sacked as Newcastle boss

"I am sure we'll see pictures of Sam in his speedos walking along a beach somewhere. That won't be a pretty sight.

Wigan manager Steve Bruce was keen for Sam Allardyce to return to work quickly

"I played with Ron [Atkinson] in about a hundred reserve games. And according to Ron, he was Man of the Match in 99 of them."

Former Aston Villa player Dennis Jackson on his contemporary Ron Atkinson

"He invented the banana shot. Trouble was, he was trying to shoot straight."

Ron returns the compliment with regard to Jackson's shooting abilities

"I'll never be able to achieve what Tommy Docherty did and take Aston Villa into the Third Division and Manchester United into the Second Division."

Ron Atkinson puts the boot in

"There will have to be a bubonic plague for me to pick Di Canio."

Giovanni Trapattoni

"This is an unusual Scotland side because they have good players."
Javler Clemente on the under 21s

"Robert Lee was able to do some running on his groin for the first time."
Glenn Hoddle

"His management style seems to be based on chaos theory."
Mark McGhee on Barry Fry

"When you finish playing football, young man, which is going to be very soon, I feel, you'll make a very good security guard."
David Pleat advises a 17-year-old Neil Ruddock

"The day I got married, Teddy Sheringham asked for a transfer. I spent my honeymoon in a hotel room with a fax machine trying to sign a replacement."
Gerry Francis

"Our central defenders, Doherty and Anthony Gardner, were fantastic and I told them that when they go to bed tonight they should think of each other."
David Pleat

"I can't imagine him jumping for the ball. One of his false eyelashes might come out."
George Graham on Tomas Brolin, the multi-million misfit he inherited from Howard Wilkinson in 1998

"He said just two words to me
in six months – you're fired!"
Tomas Brolin on George Graham

"George Graham was telling Lee Chapman
that if footballers looked after themselves
there was no reason they could not play until
35. Then he looked over to me and said,
'Well, maybe not you, Quinny.'"
Niall Quinn on his old Arsenal boss

"You sold yourself easier
than a bloody prostitute."
**Manchester City manager Joe Mercer
not impressed with Dave Bacuzzi being
given the run-around by Cardiff's
Ronnie Bird back in 1966**

"You're not a good player. In fact, you're a bad player. But I could make you into a fair player."
Malcolm Allison introduces himself to Franny Lee in 1967

"He can't head it! He can't pass it! He's no good on his left foot!"
Malcolm Allison attempting to put other managers off as they watch a young Colin Bell play for Bury as Manchester City frantically tried to raise the necessary funds in 1966

"You're not a real manager unless you've been sacked."
Malcolm Allison

"I've told the players we need to win – so that I can have the cash to buy some new ones."

Chris Turner motivates his team

"He took his curiosity to extremes: it was not unknown for Struth to carry out simple surgical procedures himself on terrified footballers laid out on the dressing-room table at Ibrox."

Journalist Alex Murphy remembers Rangers manager Bill Struth

"It was my first-ever game against Celtic and Tommy Burns kept giving me encouragement, saying that I was having a good match and to keep it going. I couldn't believe it!"

Rangers' Derek Ferguson on unusually sporting behaviour during a Glasgow derby

"Scottish football is full of hammer-throwers."

Graeme Souness

"There are two ways of getting the ball.
One is from your own team-mates, and
that's the only way."

Terry Venables

"I've been asked that question for the
last six months. It is not fair to expect me to
make such a fast decision on something that
has been put upon me like that."

**Terry Venables on whether he would remain
England manager after Euro 96**

"You get bunches of players like you do bananas, though that is a bad comparison."
Kevin Keegan

"By the look of him he must have headed a lot of balls."
Harry Redknapp on Iain Dowie

"Have I got anything bad to say about him? Well, he got cautioned by the referee at Burnley once."
West Ham manager John Lyall on Trevor Brooking

"He floats like a butterfly - and stings like one."

Brian Clough has no problem finding something bad to say about Brooking

"You could literally throw a handkerchief over the 22 outfield players."

John Gregory

"I've just been given a video recording of the game and I'm going to tape Neighbours over it."

Harry Redknapp is not happy with West Ham's goalless draw with Southampton in 1995

"I like the look of Mourinho. There's a bit of the young Clough about him. For a start he's good-looking..."
Brian Clough in November 2004

"People are comparing him [Mourinho] to Brian Clough, but Cloughy had the sexual attraction of a plate."
Journalist and author Hunter Davies

"For John Terry to die on the pitch would be glory. You would need to kill him and maybe even then he'd still play."
'Big' Phil Scolari

"They had a dozen corners, maybe 12,
I'm guessing."
Craig Brown

"I'm a firm believer that if the other side scores
first you have to score twice to win."
**Long-serving manager and FA Technical
Director, Howard Wilkinson**

"A contract on a piece of paper, saying you
want to leave, is like a piece of paper saying
you want to leave."
John Hollins

"I've got more points on my licence."
Paul Jewell on Derby's league position

"In terms of the Richter scale this was a Force 8 gale."

John Lyall confuses his scales

"There are two great teams in Liverpool: Liverpool and Liverpool Reserves."

Bill Shankly

"If Everton were playing at the bottom of my garden, I'd draw the curtains."

Bill Shankly

"Don't worry, Alan. You'll be playing near a great side."

Bill Shankly to Alan Ball after he joined Everton

"Give them these when they arrive

- they'll need them!"

**Bill Shankly hands a box of toilet
rolls to the Anfield doorman before
Everton arrive for a derby game**

"With him at centre-half, we could play Arthur
Askey in goal!"

Bill Shankly on giant defender Ron Yeats

"Take that poof bandage off, and what do
you mean you've hurt your knee? It's
Liverpool's knee!"

Bill Shankly to an injured Tommy Smith

"Tommy Smith would start a
riot in a graveyard."
Bill Shankly

"Our first goal was pure textile."
Partick Thistle great, John Lambie

"It's the equivalent to being with the prettiest
woman in the world and only sleeping with her
once a month. I prefer to sleep with someone
slightly less pretty every night!"
**Gérard Houllier's way of saying he didn't
want the England job**

"Tore's got a groin strain and he's
been playing with it."
Alex McLeish

"In football, you can never say anything is certain. The benchmark is 38-40 points. That has always been the case. That will never change."

Steve Bruce

"We're in a dogfight and the fight in the dog will get us out of trouble. We are solid behind each other, and through being solid we will get out of trouble and, if that fails, then we will be in trouble, but that's not the situation here. We'll all get in the same rowing boat, and we'll all pick up an oar and we'll row the boat."

Sir Bobby Robson in Churchillian mode at Newcastle United in 2003

"We're developing our youth policy."

Kenny Dalglish after Ian Rush joined fellow veteran John Barnes at Newcastle United

"We tried everything to get him. Maybe they offered Sharon Stone."

Tottenham Hotspur manager Ossie Ardiles on failing to get Philippe Albert, signed by Kevin Keegan for Newcastle United

"You never sell the fur of a bear before you shoot it. I have brought my cannon with me."

A cryptic Ruud Gullit on his bid to sign French winger Ibrahim Ba

"If you can't stand the heat in the dressing room, get out of the kitchen."

Terry Venables

"An inch or two either side of the post and it would have been a goal."

Dave "Harry" Bassett

"In football, if you stand still you go backwards."

Peter Reid

"The lads ran their socks into the ground."

Sir Alex Ferguson on footwear issues at Manchester United

"We threw our dice into the ring and turned up trumps."
Bruce Rioch takes a gamble

"The spirit he has shown has been second to none."
Terry Venables on defender Terry Fenwick's drink-driving charge

"To be really happy, we must throw our hearts over the bar and hope that our bodies will follow."
Graham Taylor

"Give him his head and he'll take it with both hands or feet."
Bobby Gould

"Cole should be scoring from those distances,
but I'm not going to single him out."
Sir Alex Ferguson

"We're going to start the game at nil-nil and go
out and try to get some goals."
Bryan Robson keeps it simple

"As we say in football, it'll go down
to the last wire."
Colin Todd

"Their football was exceptionally good

- and they played some good football."

Sir Bobby Robson

"And I honestly believe we can go all the way

to Wembley - unless somebody knocks us out."

Dave Bassett

"It's understandable and I understand that."

Terry Venables

"Outside of quality we had other qualities."

Arsenal great, Bertie Mee

"To be talking about vital games at this stage of the season is ridiculous, really, but tomorrow's game is absolutely vital."
Brian Horton

"What I said to them at half-time would be unprintable on the radio."
Gerry Francis

"If we played like this every week we wouldn't be so inconsistent."
Bryan Robson puts his finger on it

"I promise results, not promises."
John Bond

"Without picking out anyone in particular,
I thought Mark Wright was tremendous."
Graeme Souness

"Klinsmann has taken to English football
like a duck out of water."
Gerry Francis on the German striker

"Even when you're dead, you must never
allow yourself just to lie down and be buried."
Gordon Lee plans a comeback

"We ended up playing football,
and that's not our style."
Alex MacDonald

"Hagi is a brilliant player, but we're not going to get psychedelic over him."

Andy Roxburgh rules out a summer of love approach against Romania

"It's thrown a spanner in the fire."

Bobby Gould

"Home advantage gives you an advantage."

Sir Bobby Robson

"...when Flitcroft played for the A team, he had 'footballer' written all over his forehead."

Colin Bell on what marked Garry Flitcroft out from the rest

"I can count on the fingers of one hand ten games where we've caused our own downfall."

Joe Kinnear

"If it had gone in, it would have been a goal."

Joe Royle

"I am often interested in players but I never say so, although I am looking for a striker and a midfield player."

Colin Todd keeps his cards close to his chest

"Obviously six points from four games is worth more than four points from four games so I'm not going to make myself a mathematical idiot."

Fulham boss Roy Hodgson keeps things simple

"We are not putting our cape over the tunnel: we are putting our cape in the tunnel."

Howard Wilkinson

"The way forwards is backwards."

Dave Sexton

"I like to think it's a case of crossing the 'i's and dotting the t's."

Dave Bassett

"When you score one goal more than the other team in a cup tie it is always enough."

Former Italy coach and father of Milan great, Paolo, Cesare Maldini

"What he's got is legs, which the other midfielders don't have."
Lennie Lawrence

"Hartson's got more previous than Jack the Ripper."
Harry Redknapp

"The important thing is he shook hands with us over the phone."
Alan Ball

"When a player gets to 30, so does his body."
Glenn Hoddle

"I have a number of alternatives and each one gives me something different."
Glenn Hoddle

"With hindsight, it's easy to look at it with hindsight."
Glenn Hoddle

"When I heard the draw I was out on the golf course. I had an eight-iron in one hand and my mobile in the other. When we came out with United, my club went further than the ball."
Harry Redknapp reacts to the FA Cup draw

"I just wonder what would have happened if the shirt had been on the other foot."
Mike Walker

"Some of our players have got no brains, so I've given them the day off tomorrow to rest them."

David Kemp

"The beauty of cup football is that Jack always has a chance of beating Goliath."

Terry Butcher rewrites the Bible

"Of the nine red cards this season we probably deserved half of them."

Arsène Wenger

"We didn't look like scoring, although we looked like we were going to get a goal."

Alan Buckley

"We're down to the bare knuckles."

The ever-combative George Graham

"Davor has a left leg and a nose in the box."

Arsène Wenger on his Croatian striker

"Today's top players only want to play in London or for Manchester United. That's what happened when I tried to sign Alan Shearer and he went to Blackburn."

Graeme Souness

"I don't read everything I read in the press."

Dave Jones

"We are now entering a new millennium and football's a completely different cup of tea."

Dave Bassett

"I was a young lad when I was growing up."

David O'Leary

"It would be foolish to believe that automatic promotion is automatic in any way whatsoever."

Dave Bassett

"I was inbred into the game by my father."

A disturbing one from David Pleat

"If it comes to penalties, one of these two great sides could go out on the whim of a ball."
Peter Shreeves

"In football, time and space are the same thing."
Graham Taylor shows his scientific side

"Very few of us have any idea whatsoever of what life is like living in a goldfish bowl - except, of course, for those of us who are goldfish."
Graham Taylor

"We can't behave like crocodiles and cry over spilled milk and broken eggs."
Giovanni Trapattoni

"I've seen players sent off for worse than that."

Joe Royle

"The margin is very marginal."

Sir Bobby Robson

"I'm not superstitious or anything like that,

but I'll just hope we'll play our best and

put it in the lap of the gods."

Terry Neill, not superstitious

"We are really quite lucky this year

because Christmas falls on Christmas Day."

Bobby Gould with some festive cheer

"Being given chances and not taking them. That's what life is all about."

Ron Greenwood

"I felt a lump in my mouth as the ball went in."

A classic from Terry Venables

"Tim Sherwood has come in, done very well and given us another string to the bow in a different type of way."

Glenn Hoddle

"He should pack it in now. He'll have 100% record and win Manager of the Month!"

Kevin Keegan on West Ham's caretaker manager Trevor Brooking

"If we start counting our chickens before they hatch, they won't lay any eggs in the basket."
Sir Bobby Robson

"Playing another London side could be an omen, but I don't believe in omens."
George Graham

"It will be a once-in-a-lifetime experience that doesn't come along that often."
Steve McLaren on FC Twente's Champions League draw against Arsenal

"We played a 4-4-3 formation, which we have played before and never failed to win with it."
Mark McGhee's new system looks like a winner

"Referees don't come down here with

a particular-flavoured shirt on."

Steve Coppell

"We are not a team of girls."

Real Madrid boss Vincente Del Bosque

refutes allegations that his team will

struggle against a physical Manchester

United side

"We are a young side that will only get younger."

Paul Hart

"You can't say my team aren't winners.

They've proved that by finishing fourth,

third and second in the last three years."

Gérard Houllier

"We changed to a back four and went 4-4-3."

Glenn Hoddle adopts Mark McGhee's extra player formation

"Alan is struggling to walk and he can't use crutches because his hand is in plaster. We may have to put him in a wheelchair."

Bobby Robson's medical assessment on Alan Shearer

"I'd go home and kick the cat if I could - but I haven't got one."

Doncaster's Sean O'Driscoll

"Although we are playing Russian Roulette
we are obviously playing Catch 22 at the
moment and it's a difficult scenario to
get my head round."
Paul Sturrock is not alone

"We're actually thinking that Snow White can
lead them out. And I'm being serious."
**Celtic's Gordon Strachan worries about
his side's chances against a much taller
Manchester United team**

"I can't see us getting beat now,
once we get our tails in front."
Jim Platt

"If I had knocked on it I would probably have had it slapped back in my face!"

Zat Knight on whether he'd spoken with Martin O'Neill about his lack of first-team opportunities at Aston Villa

"After you've scored a goal it's just orgasmic ... if you asked me just after a game I'd says its better than sex, but if you asked me just after sex I'd say, 'Forget it, mate.'"

Trevor Sinclair on scoring

Chapter Four:
FOOTBALL
CRAZY TALK

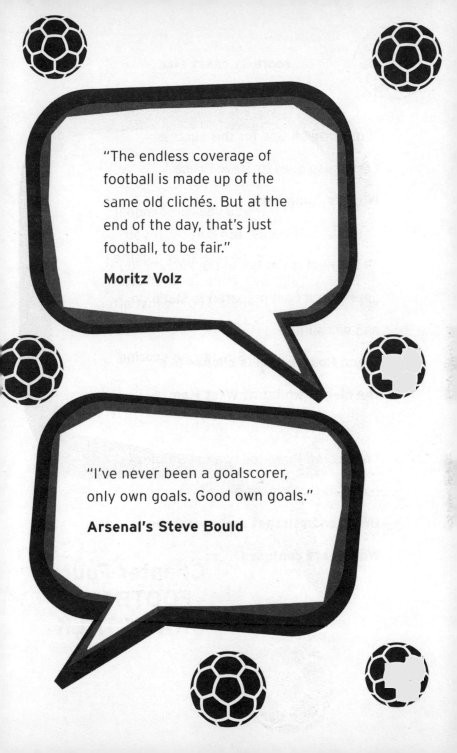

"The endless coverage of football is made up of the same old clichés. But at the end of the day, that's just football, to be fair."

Moritz Volz

"I've never been a goalscorer, only own goals. Good own goals."

Arsenal's Steve Bould

"I must thank God for this success.
Credit also goes to Steve Bruce."
Wigan's Amir Zaki

"If the heat is too hot in the kitchen you
get out, but I am prepared to stand up
and be counted."
**Glenn Roeder avoids cliches like
the plague whilst at West Ham**

"We scored three today and 99 times
out of 10 that means a win."
**Brighton assistant manager Dean
White gets confused**

'I must admit I have a dressing room curiosity over Beckham. I want to see if he is equipped as he is in the underwear adverts."
Marco Borriello looks forward to the arrival of his new teammate at AC Milan

"I don't know what state of mind his body's in."
Jamie Redknapp on Stoke's Ricardo Fuller

"Natural managers do not exist, I have never met one. If a natural manager exists, he must be in paradise."
Arsene Wenger

"Backsides and opinions, we;ve all got them but it's not always a good idea to air them in public."
Mick McCarthy

"They've kicked our backsides, we've got to lick our wounds..."
Nice. Steve Bruce

"I've always believed at this time of the season you get to see people like oranges - you squeeze them and some of them tend to capitulate."
Aidy Boothroyd

"I think it's fair to say we're an improving team and a team that's getting better."
Everton skipper Phil Neville

"Apparently when you head a football, you lose brain cells, but it doesn't bother me... I'm a horse. No one's proved it yet have they?"
David May

"Well, I rose like a salmon at the far post, but Pally rose like a fresher salmon and towered above me, headed the ball at the keeper, the keeper fumbled, then I saw a sudden flash of brilliant red and leathered it into the roof of the net with my left foot sponsored by Diadora boots."
David May's vivid description of his goal in Manchester United's 4-0 win over Porto.

"The White Pelé? You're more like the White Nellie!"
Bill Shankly as Peter Thompson struggled to reproduce his international form in Brazil on the domestic stage

"Gary Neville is the club captain but he has been injured for the best part of a year now – and Giggsy's taken up the mantlepiece."
Rio Ferdinand

"My dad does know Romeo from the group and he's played in a few bands with him. But my dad was definitely not the drummer in Showaddywaddy."
Dion Dublin debunks a great football myth

"I would not sign for another club, not even for 15 million dollars. However, it would be different if they were to instead offer me 15 different women from all around the world. I would tell the club chairman: 'Please let me make these women happy – I will satisfy them like they have never been satisfied before.'"

Sasa Curcic lays down his terms
for a move away from Aston Villa

"Aston Villa! What suburb of Rome is Aston Villa from?

Tom Hanks – not a soccer fan

"I'll get in trouble with my girlfriend if I play
– I don't think she'll be too happy if I'm
chasing Totti all over Rome."
**Jonathan Woodgate on his chances of
making only his second start for Leeds
United, away to AS Roma in the UEFA
Cup in 1998**

"The neighbours on one side have got a villa
in Portugal, the other side have got a house in
America. We're looking for one in Filey."
David Batty

"I am quite a gruesome person. I did have a
scrapbook on the Yorkshire Ripper... That was
one of my most treasured possessions."
David Batty

"I'm very passionate about antiques because they are like people. You can learn a lot from them."

Emmanuel Petit

Police officer: "Mr McCoist, do you have a police record?"

Ian Durrant: "'Walking on the Moon'..."

From Ian Durrant's autobiography

"If, as some people think, there is such a thing as reincarnation, I'd love to come back as an eagle. I love the way eagles move, the way they soar, the way they gaze."

Eric Cantona

Interviewer: "What do you say to the rumour that Gary Neville has been stealing bodies from graveyards and building some kind of creature from the parts in his garage?"

Denis Irwin: "I don't think it's Nev. He just lays up in his house all day. If you'd said any other player then maybe…"

A spoof interviewer from the Mick Molloy Show livens up a Manchester United press call in Australia in summer 1999

"Luca [Vialli] thinks he looks like Bruce Willis, but I think he looks more like Bruce Forsyth."

Aaron Lincoln, Chelsea kitman in 1999

"I'll tell you what my real dream is. I mean my absolute number one dream that will mean I die a happy man if it happens. I want to see a UFO. They're real. I don't care if you look at me like that. UFOs are a definite fact and I've got to see one soon."

Paul Gascoigne bewilders some journalists

"In English, the things you use in casinos are chips, but in Italian we call them fish. So I once said, 'When the fish are down...' Everybody was, like, 'What are you talking about?'"

Gianluca Vialli on his attempts to conquer the local lingo

"Every time I see him it reminds me to buy a pint of milk on the way home."

More from Aaron Lincoln, this time on striker Mikael Forssell's pale features

"A survey was conducted of the world's female population asking them if they would sleep with Bill Clinton. 80 per cent of them answered, 'What, again?'"

Peter Schmeichel tells a joke

"John Bond has blackened my name with his insinuations about the private lives of football managers. Both my wives are upset."

Malcolm Allison

"On the pitch, when I see green or smell green, I get a little bit crazy. The grass, you know? I get this green mist."
Jimmy Floyd Hasselbaink

"After you've scored a goal it's just orgasmic ... if you asked me just after a game I'd says its better than sex, but if you asked me just after sex I'd say, 'Forget it, mate.'"
Trevor Sinclair on scoring
– one way or the other

"The thing about sport, any sport, is that swearing is very much part of it."
Jimmy Greaves

"You've got to take the rough with the smooth. It's like love and hate, war and peace, all that boll*cks."
A bit of philosophy from Ian Wright

"Dogs are very honest. They'll never let you down. They'll play football with you in the garden ... and at the end they'll crap all over your lawn."
Mark Viduka

"I've seen myself referred to as 'a legend'. I've been called worse, let's put it that way."
Robbie Fowler

"I'd certainly like to be as, er,
big as Lara Croft one day."
**Michael Owen at the launch of
his own computer game**

"I would like to be in a movie. I want to be
the bad person who is killed at the end of the
movie, like Gary Oldman in Air Force One."
Frank Leboeuf

"It won't be long before he has our
supporters hanging from the rafters."
**Alan Ball predicting a bright future
for new signing Gio Kinkladze in 1995**

"My mother wanted me to be a folk dancer, so when my father went to Russia to work for three years she hid away my football boots and took me to dancing classes."
Gio Kinkladze

"Sorry, Mr Chairman, but this is the earliest I have been late for some time."
Ally McCoist apologizes to Rangers chairman David Murray

"No comment, lads – and that's off the record."
Ally McCoist to a group of reporters during a Rangers media ban

"I'm often asked how this Rangers team compares with the Lisbon Lions. I have to be honest and say I think it would be a draw but, then, some of us are getting on for 60."

Glasgow Celtic great, Bertie Auld in 1993, after city rivals Rangers had reached the group stage of the Champions League for the first time

"We like Scotland because we love shortbread. Coming here is interesting to him."

Nivaldo Baldo, adviser to Brazilian Celtic trialist Marcio Amoroso back in 2004

"We signed to play until the day we died,

and we did."

Jimmy Greaves speaks on radio,

not from beyond the grave

"Two things struck me straight away.

The standard of José's English and the

fact that he was a nice-looking boy.

Too good-looking for my liking."

Sir Bobby Robson on Mourinho

"The moral of the story is not to listen to those

who tell you not to play the violin but to play

the tambourine."

José Mourinho has a Cantona moment

"I speak a bit of English so in the dressing room I knew that Mourinho's translations weren't literal. It was Robson, plus Mourinho's own observations. And they made sense."
Former Barcelona player Oscar Garcia reveals how José Mourinho dealt with the difficult job of translating for Sir Bobby Robson

"I've never been a goalscorer, only own goals. Good own goals."
Arsenal's Steve Bould

"As far as I'm concerned, Tony [Adams] is like the Empire State Building."
Ian Wright

"To play for the club you support is a dream come true."

Ashley Cole on Arsenal before the dream turned sour

"Bottle is a quality too, you know. It's not just about ball control and being clever. Sometimes you have to show the world what's between your legs."

Graeme Souness

"As the ball came over, I remembered what Graham Taylor said about my having no right foot, so I headed it in."

John Barnes scoring against Taylor's Aston Villa in a 1988 FA Cup tie

"The best Italian this club has
signed is the chef."
Frank Leboeuf on Chelsea

"Nobody hands you cups on a plate."
**Terry McDermott, assistant to Kevin
Keegan at Newcastle United**

"She [Eileen Drewery] gives the
players a shoulder to talk to."
Neil Webb

"Short back and sides."
**Unidentified England player to Glenn
Hoddle's faith healer Eileen Drewery**

"Once you've had a bull terrier, you never want another dog. I've got six bull terriers, a Rottweiler and a bulldog."
Julian Dicks

"He'd no alternative but to make a needless tackle."
Chelsea and Celtic defender Paul Elliott

"I was disappointed to leave Spurs, but quite pleased that I did."
Steve Perryman

"I spent four indifferent years at Goodison, but they were great years."
Martin Hodge

"I always used to put my right boot on first,

and then obviously my right sock."

Barry Venison

"I can't even remember when the Seventies was."

Robbie Keane

"You don't need balls to play in a cup final."

Steve Claridge

"I was born in Newcastle and I've played

for Newcastle Schoolboys all my life."

The forever-young Dennis Tueart

"Paul Scholes – the most complete mental player I've ever seen."

Former Manchester United trainee Ben Thornley

"I'm as happy as I can be – but I have been happier."

Aston Villa and Middlesbrough defender Ugo Ehiogu

"I find the growing intervention by the football authorities in strictly footballing matters a rather worrying trend."

Kenny Cunningham wishes the FA would stay out of football

"You can't do better than a goal
on your first start."
Bobby Zamora

"I took a whack on my left ankle, but
something told me it was my right."
Lee Hendrie

"Left alone with our own heads on,
we can be pretty mental."
Tony Adams

"I faxed a transfer request to the club at the
beginning of the week, but let me state that
I don't want to leave Leicester."
Stan Collymore

"I was surprised, but I always say nothing surprises me in football."

Les Ferdinand

"I was watching the Blackburn game on TV on Sunday when it flashed on the screen that George [Ndah] had scored in the first minute at Birmingham. My first reaction was to ring him up. Then I remembered he was out there playing."

Ade Akinbiyi

"He'll be the leader in the tool kit."

Robbie Earle doesn't say which tool it is

"We could be putting the hammer

in Luton's coffin."

Ray Wilkins

"The Championship is the carrot

at the end of the Championship."

Tony Cottee

"It was a game of two halves, literally."

Chris Powell

"It's a no-win game for us. Although

I suppose we can win by winning."

Gary Doherty

"I was both surprised and delighted to take the armband for both legs."

Gary O'Neil

"I've always been a childhood Liverpool fan, even when I was a kid."

Harry Kewell

"He's started anticipating what's going to happen before it's even happened."

Graeme Le Saux

"In the last ten minutes I was breathing out of my ar*e."

Clinton Morrison

"Now the world is my lobster."

Keith O'Neill

"We feel unbeatable at Ewood Park

- even when we play away."

David Bentley loses his bearings

"I've got way too many cars - six here and
the others in America. I get up in the morning
and decide which one to drive. Most people
wouldn't call them classic cars - most people
would call them pieces of crap."

**Reading's Marcus Hahnemann will never
make it as a second-hand car salesman**

"I am not going to leave. Never. I am staying here for life."

Thierry Henry stays put at Arsenal
- before he signs for Barcelona

"I'm not sure what the disagreement was because those who voted for it were pretty unanimous."

Sir Trevor Brooking needs a dictionary

"Had I not become a footballer, I think I would have been a virgin."

At least Peter Crouch is honest

"He's had three offside decisions, two right, two wrong."

Chris Kamara's argument just doesn't add up

"The fire is always ready, but now it looks as though you're burned on the village green quicker than ever."
Arsene Wenger on football's sacrificial tendencies

"Ten years ago a playmaker could only play when they had the ball. Not now."
Joe Cole on the art of invisible passing

"Crime levels are really high in London. I would not feel comfortable about leaving my wife and children alone at home."
Jens Lehmann endears himself to Londoners

"Arsenal are without doubt the best league in the Premiership."

Sam Allardyce gets it wrong

"Well I'm 28 now and people say you reach your peak at 28, so hopefully I've got my best years ahead of me."

Kieron Dyer

"Without being too harsh on David Beckham, he cost us the match."

Ian Wright is a little harsh

"The big thing about Newcastle is there is only Newcastle in Newcastle."

Joey Barton was always top of his geography class

"We're in pole position in second place."

David Healy isn't a natural front-runner

"At the moment we're not playing like a top six side. To be a top six side, you've wgot to be in the top six."

You can't fault Jamie Scowcroft's logic

"Shocks can happen when you expect them least."

Dundee United's Willo Flood states the obvious

"Most goals go between the posts."

Peter Beagrie is spot on

Interviewer: "How do you say screamer
in French?"
Wenger: "I'm sorry, I can't speak French
any more!"
Arsene Wenger loses the plot

"We will probably have to score more goals
than we let in to win games."
Jermaine Jenas has a cunning plan

"If it's anywhere on the pitch apart from inside
the 18-yard box, you'd get a penalty."
Chris Kamara wants more spot kicks

"I'm 30 now but back then I was 19... that's
seven years ago."
Lee Bowyer mislays four years of his life

"England did nothing in the World Cup, so why are they bringing books out? We've got beat in the quarter-final, here's my book. Who wants to read that? I don't."
Joey Barton isn't big on books

"Next year I'm sure Arsenal fans would prefer 1-0 draws."
5 Live's Spoony really should know better

"Alex Ferguson is the best manager I've ever had at this level. Well, he's the only manager I've actually had at this level. But he's the best manager I've ever had."
David Beckham trips over his own tongue

"I wouldn't say it's a must-win, but it's definitely a game we need to win."

Peter Crouch definitely doesn't want to lose

"I've worked my nuts off to get here. My groin's a bit sore."

What did Michael Owen expect?

"I've had an interest in racing all my life, or longer really."

Kevin Keegan was a foetal fan of the sport of kings

"Before the game, Naomi Campbell came into our dressing room and saw a few things."

QPR's Dexter Blackstock welcomes catwalk royalty

"That was in the past – we're in the future now."
David Beckham fancies himself as the new Doctor Who

"It's been harder this year. Liverpool have got better, Man United have got better, Arsenal have got better, and Tottenham have joined the quartet of five teams."
Joe Cole was never any good as maths

"He's going to be what? Oh for God's sake! Sir David Beckham? You're having a laugh. He's just a good footballer with a famous bird."
Ian Holloway is Beckham's biggest fan

"Glen Johnson can't help being good-looking - he was born like that."

Harry Redknapp watches his players from a young age

"Andy Johnson has been playing up front on his own with James Beattie all season."

Alan Shearer on Everton's solitary duo

"Jealousy is the weapon of the incompetent and frustrated. It all makes me rewind the cassette of my life and remind me who I was."

Jose Mourinho has an Eric Cantona moment

"If that wasn't a goal, my auntie's my uncle!"

Chris Kamara unwittingly reveals a dark family secret

"I nicked a sheep in Reading once.

That was mad."

Maybe John Hartson should be

deported Down Under

"Almunia took the criticism and responded with

one word - his performance on the pitch."

Arsene Wenger uses five words instead of one

"I consider myself a normal kind of bloke.

I get up in the morning and go to the toilet."

Michael Owen provides a little too much

insight into his domestic routine

"John Terry is a bloke."

It's impossible to pull the wool

over Ray Wilkins' eyes

"We've ended the season on a high – apart from the last game, which we lost."

David Beckham's glass is always half full

"I didn't want to talk to people for three weeks after the defeat. I touched my wife but didn't speak to her."

Martin Jol is an old romantic at heart

"I don't fight about girlfriends. I have lots of them and I'm married."

Portsmouth's Benjani Mwaruwari drops himself right in it

"We are happy with the three points, but it could have been more."

Ryan Giggs is never satisfied

"It's like The Witches of Eastwick. They need Jack Nicholson to come in and sort them right out."

Ian Holloway is glued to Big Brother

"Agbonlahor had a great chance, but really it wasn't a great chance."

Alan Smith can't make his mind up

"I can assure West Ham fans that no stone will be unearthed in our preparation for next week."

Alan Pardew doesn't care about training

"The 2,000 away fans will be unhappy. In fact half of them have gone, there's only 500 left."

Chris Waddle misplaces 500 Man City supporters

"Fourth place is what we're aiming for. We don't want to be second best."
Phil Neville sets his sights high

"I not only like to have the TV and light on to help me sleep, but also a vacuum cleaner. Failing that, a fan or a hairdryer will do. I've ruined so many hairdryers by letting them burn out. So far I haven't set fire to anywhere."
The strange nocturnal habits of
Wayne Rooney

"We don't talk about going higher than fifth, we just want to play well. Then with a bit of luck we can go higher than fifth."
Tottenham's Kevin-Prince Boateng
forgets himself

"Home advantage is usually an advantage
to the home team."
Johnny Giles tells it like it is

"Glenn Roeder will think for a few minutes
before making a rash decision."
Steve Stone, with touching faith

"At this level, you cannot defend like that and
get away with it. We've defended like that and
got away with it today."
Even Steve Bruce thinks he's talking rubbish

"It's when Paul Scholes isn't playing that
Manchester United miss him."
The genius of ex-Red Devil Arthur Albiston

"We wanted to keep it quiet, and didn't make an issue of it. We went through the proper channels and hoped it would die a death."
Steve Coppell sensitively plays down death threats to two of his players

"If you're dealing with someone who's only wearing underpants. you're better off giving him some trousers."
Arsene Wenger embarrasses easily

"I have a feeling it's the bottom three who will go down."
Graham Taylor should go with his feelings

"Every dog has its day – and today is woof day!"
The one and only Ian Holloway

"Chelsea have scored in every game this season and they'll need to keep that record up to win today."

Jamie Redknapp knows how to win a match

"I had 15 messages after the game. The best one was from my mum, which said, 'Come outside and get some sweets'!"

Manchester City's Nedum Onuoha still has a sweet tooth

"This has been our Achilles heel which has been stabbing us in the back all season."

David O'Leary, anatomical genius

"A contract on a piece of paper, saying
you want to leave, is like a piece of paper
saying you want to leave."
It's all black and white to John Hollins

"I did not have any nerves, although I did
go to the toilet just before I came on so
there might have been some there."
**Theo Walcott conjures up an
unsavoury image**

"My ankle injury's been a real pain in the arse."
**Southampton's David Prutton failed his
biology GCSE**

"Any manager will tell you they'd rather win one and lose two than draw three because you get more points."

Les Ferdinand needs a calculator

"When Jason Koumas is on form, he's the type of player who calls all the strings."

Ian Rush reckons Jason Koumas is something of a rope charmer

"This performance today shows that other teams are going to have to score more goals than us if they want to beat us."

No-one pulls the wool over Darren Bent's eyes

"People just looked lost. Too many players looked like fish on trees."

Paul Merson on England's worrying failings

"If I put a cap on, people say, 'It's Peter Crouch with a cap on'."

Peter Crouch is master of disguise

"Unfortunately, we keep kicking ourselves in the foot."

Ray Wilkins knows exactly where the England Under-21 players are going wrong

"When I read a few things, I smell a few coats."

Jose Mourinho should go to the doctor

"I'd like to be a seagull who hasn't been to the toilet for a month and is waiting above Sean Davis' head when he comes out of the shower."
Matt Taylor probably needs counselling

"I listen to 50 Cent, Jay-Z, Stereophonics, Arctic Monkeys, also the musical Oliver - I can sing every tune."
Wayne Rooney reveals too much

"People laughed when David Hasselhoff tried to claim that Baywatch had played a part in bringing peace to the world but I think he had a point."
And you though Moritz Volz just watched it for the swimsuits

"People just looked lost. Too many players looked like fish on trees."

Paul Merson on England's worrying failings

"I do not think about the national team too much because footballistically it is not of too much interest."

Arsene Wenger invents a new word

"Leeds is a great club and it's been my home for years, even though I live in Middlesbrough."

Jonathan "Two Homes" Woodgate

"I don't think we threatened the Arse at all today."

Roy Hodgson wanted more from his team at the Emirates

"Cristiano Ronaldo has a left foot, a right foot – the list is endless."
Steve Coppell is simply in awe of the two-footed Man United star

"Jermain [Defoe] is only five foot but he was about eight foot before the game."
Robbie Keane on his incredible shrinking team-mate

"I moisturise daily with Nivea and I regularly use Nivea body lotion."
Freddie Ljungberg is nothing if not moist

"With a team you live in a tunnel and sometimes you have to go down and flirt with hell to see how much you can deal with that, so that you become stronger. But you go quickly to hell and very slowly to heaven."

Bible studies with Arsene Wenger

"I know Rafa well and he will break his own head to find a solution to get the title for Liverpool."

Pepe Reina on his head-banging boss

"I am not happy or unhappy with him."

Arsene Wenger is definitely indifferent

"We were disappointed that we conceded a goal in our dressing room."
Stuart Pearce's defence must be really, really bad...

"I haven't read it and I haven't seen the pictures but it's a fantastic book."
Maybe Sven-Goran Eriksson got the audio version?

"I was still, you know, throwing my clothes out of the pram a little bit."
Joey Barton, childhood stripper

"Why should I? I haven't done anything wrong yet."
Sam Allardyce refuses to resign

"I took a whack on my left ankle,

but something told me it was my right."

Maybe Lee Hendrie also got a whack

to the head...

"He makes players 10 feet taller."

Rob Lee on Kevin Keegan's

surprising abilities

"I'll hire a big chauffeur-driven car

so I can take my kids out for a walk."

Florent Malouda misses the point

"Nothing surprises me in football but

if I said I was astounded that would be

an understatement."

Ray Wilkins does his best to stay calm

"Danny Murphy's been scoring
with benders all season."
Bryan Robson casts aspersions

"I'm not that bloke Mystic Meg."
Rio Ferdinand clears up the confusion

"Bingo can be very exciting because you
can be waiting for a long time for just one
number to make the game complete."
Cristiano "Full House" Ronaldo

"That's what the goals are there for,
to keep the ball out."
**Lee Dixon gets "goals" and
"goalkeepers" confused**

"Van Der Sar is one of the best two-footed goalkeepers in the league."

Chris Waddle bestows a backhanded compliment

"Rooney will do anything for you in any position."

Wayne Rooney's keen to please, according to Mark Lawrenson

"Burton just couldn't lose tonight. Except that they did."

Ian Wright forgets the score

"I am a Nigerian and I will remain a Nigerian until the day I die."

Kanu is nothing if not patriotic

"In this day and age you don't see too many footballers with two feet."

Peter Allen is watching a different game to everyone else

"I usually don't have sex. Not on the same day. I say no thanks. I guess that, mentally, I want to keep the feeling in my feet and that's why. I think the feeling sort of disappears out of your feet if you have sex before. I have tried before and my feet felt like concrete when you are supposed to kick the ball."

Freddie Ljungberg likes to save his energy

"It's a tough month for Liverpool over the next five or six weeks."

Alan Green needs to check his calendar

"I was a bit anxious when I got to the stadium, but in all fairness if hadn't been anxious, I'd have been worried."
Paul Robinson finds it hard to relax

"I was both surprised and delighted to take the armband for both legs."
Gary O'Neil reveals his inexperience in the art of captaincy

"We have bought two new players. One is younger than the other."
Sven-Goran Eriksson never signs twins

"The endless coverage of football is made up of the same old clichés. But at the end of the day, that's just football, to be fair."

Moritz Volz, master of the self-fulfilling prophecy

"People need to understand what kind of goldfish Wayne Rooney lives in."

Graham Taylor knows something we don't

"I think they'll have to throw the kitchen sink at them now a bit. Maybe not the whole sink, with all the plumbing – maybe just the taps for now."

David Pleat urges caution

**Chapter Four:
SAY WHAT?**

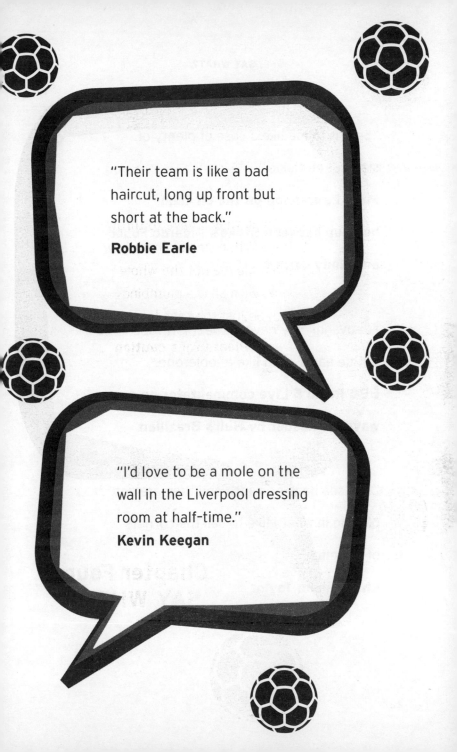

"Their team is like a bad haircut, long up front but short at the back."
Robbie Earle

"I'd love to be a mole on the wall in the Liverpool dressing room at half-time."
Kevin Keegan

"Seems to me like a case of plenty of slap but no tickle."

Mark Lawrenson on the on-field bust-up between Stoke's Ricardo Fuller and Andy Griffin

"Geovanni may have a sweet left foot but he has a head like a toblerone."

BBC Radio 5 Live commentator on a wayward header by Hull's Brazilian

"Chelsea have no width and they are not playing in what I like to call the corners of the pitch."

Eh? Graham Taylor

"That goal surprised most people, least of all myself."
Garth Crooks

"He's a big unit - and if he's Junior Agogo, I certainly wouldn't want to meet Senior Agogo."
Fox Sport's Simon Hill

"Dirk Kuyt is earning himself the reputation as Anfield's Prince Harry - in the front line for three months and no one knows about it."
Phil Thomas, *The Sun*

"Obviously Sky gets its money from prescription payers."
Martin Keown turns pundit

"Sloppy, that's the only word to describe

that pass... casual."

Andy Gray

It's never over until it's over, but this is over."

Chris Kamara

"I wouldn't trust some of these people

to walk my dog."

Roy Keane is suspicious of football pundits

"He looks like a man who has nits

and worms at the same time."

Mark Lawrenson's worrying diagnosis of

Aston Villa boss Martin O'Neill

"Scotland can't afford to take their minds off the gas."

Andy Townsend on the Tartan Army's mental fuel

"And Rush, quick as a needle..."

Ron Jones on Liverpool legend Ian

"The Italians are hoping for an Italian victory."

David Coleman hits the nail on the head

"This is the first time Denmark has ever reached the World Cup finals, so this is the most significant moment in Danish history."

John Helm

"He's multi-lingual. He'll say 'ouch' in five different languages."

Mark Lawrenson on cunning linguist Philippe Senderos

"That free-kick was so wide it nearly hit my car."

Paul Merson is worried about his no-claims bonus

"Pinpoint accuracy from Beckham there. Two inches lower and it would've been a goal."

Gerry Armstrong needs a tape measure

"Murphy was unselfish, but I feel he should have shot himself."

David Pleat is a tad harsh

"Nothing surprises me in football, nothing - but this is a bit of a surprise!"

Tommy Docherty loses the plot on Radio Manchester

"Stamford Bridge holds 42,000, so 10 per cent of that would be about 4.1 thousand."

Mike Parry's calculator goes on the blink

"Both the keepers are suffering from confidence."

Alan Shearer likes nervous goalkeepers

"A bit of pushing and shoving between Deco and Sissoko. It's like a terrier picking a fight with an Alsatian, but in this instance the terrier comes out on top as the Alsatian is booked. Obviously dogs don't get yellow cards in the park."

The BBC's Charlie Henderson unravels a canine conundrum

"You can't turn a sow's ear into a rose. Or a flower."

Mike Parry mixes his metaphors

"The one thing Cristiano Ronaldo has is pace, quick feet and a great eye for goal."

Chris Waddle has more than one thing on his mind

"They've scored 32 goals in every game this season."
Alan Parry heaps a little too much praise on Arsenal

"The next match here at the Banks's Stadium is on New Year's Day, which this year falls on January 1st."
The Walsall PA leaves nothing to chance

"Martin Jol is literally a dead man walking."
Steve Claridge thinks the Spurs boss is a zombie

"You feel for Chimbonda there. It's come off the post so fast it's in slow motion."
Eagle-eyed Glenn Hoddle

"Reina's name in Spanish means queen – and he came out like a queen there and kicked it straight at his defender."
The PC era has clearly passed Gerry Armstrong by

"At Hearts there's just a few seconds left. One thousand, four hundred and forty seconds in fact, because they kicked off late."
Jeff Stelling is a stickler for accuracy

"And here comes Crouch, like some sort of rampaging super spider."
Peter Drury has a dark imagination

"Prica has scored for Sunderland – his dad is rumoured to be called Pap."
Ian Payne spices up his commentary

"Ronaldo got into the area and had about 11 legovers."
Paul Merson on the United star's "scoring" habits

"As the old saying goes, people in glasses shouldn't throw stones."

Because they might not hit the target? Alan Smith (Snr)

"The top four sides will always be the top four sides."

Andy Gray doesn't predict big changes in the future

"Most managers would give their right arm for a European Cup, and Paisley had three."

The BBC's Manish Bhasin on the three-armed Liverpool icon

"He didn't have his body behind that one but luckily he has arms like an orang-utan."

Stuart Lovell makes a monkey of Hibs goalkeeper Yves Kalambay

"And the score is nil-nil, just as it was at the beginning of the game."

Mike Ingham has been keeping an eye on the scoreboard

"Tottenham haven't created many chances. Robbie Keane's flashed a couple of times but nothing more."

Andy Gray cops an unwanted eyeful

"Peter Schmeichel will be a father figure for Kasper (Schmeichel)."
Jamie Redknapp states the alarmingly obvious

"Liverpool are going to have to start getting results if they're going to start winning."
Andy Townsend has wise words for the Reds

"He was a dead man walking...he didn't have a leg to stand on."
Five Live's Malcolm Boyden ties himself in metaphorical knots

"The team colours of both these sides need no introduction. Tottenham are in white and Chelsea are in blue."
John Motson quickly changes his mind

"You can only score against the team you're playing against."
David Platt, tactical genius

"I see they are wearing the white of Real Madrid - that's like a red rag to a bull."
Is David Pleat colour-blind?

"He's a typical winger in that he's not brave and tackling's not a strong point – although he's not afraid to go into a tackle."
Les Ferdinand reckons Ashley Young has a split personality

"The amount that Chelsea have missed Petr Cech can't be overplayed – although Jose Mourinho has overplayed it."
Peter Beagrie can't quite make his mind up

"Only Arsenal have scored more goals than Arsenal this season."
Dickie Davies can't get the Gunners off his mind

"The alarm bells are flashing."

Rob Hawthorne witnesses a sound and light spectacular

"In this league, any team can beat any other – and to prove it there were seven draws yesterday."

Don Goodman's theory falls distinctly flat

"There's only one person who knows how he missed that, and that's Wayne Rooney, and even he doesn't know."

George Graham searches for answers

"Riise's had four chances. I wouldn't say
two of them were chances, mind."
Andy Gray confuses himself

"By trying to sign Peter Crouch, are
Middlesbrough aiming too high?"
Jeff Stelling, stand-up comedian

"It's like the Sea of Galilee – the
two defenders just parted."
Mark Lawrenson gets all Biblical

"We did wonder about the possibility
of a Spurs versus Tottenham draw."
**Matt Smith does his best to confuse
the ITV audience**

"There is a no-smoking policy in all parts of the Layer Road ground. Anyone who is caught smoking will be taken away, strapped to an electric chair and electrocuted until they are dead. Thank you."

The Colchester stadium announcer makes his point

"There's a certain Englishness about the English game."

Fair comment from Alan Parry

"If Arsenal lose now, I'll eat my heart."

Craig Burley is nothing if not confident watching the Gunners take on Reading

"I think they'll have to throw the kitchen sink at them now a bit. Maybe not the whole sink, with all the plumbing - maybe just the taps for now."

David Pleat urges caution

"A handball is when your hand touches the ball."

Gary Lineker answers the question no-one was asking

"Reading just had a great five-man move that involved everyone."

Phil Thompson's figures just don't add up

"He should have been given the goal of the season for that shot, even though it went wide."

Pat Nevin fails to grasp the whole "goal of the season" concept

"If there is a qualified referee in the ground, please can he make himself known to a steward."

The waggish Fulham half-time announcer isn't impressed with the referee's performance

"Adebayor was queerly frustrated."

Does Jeff Stelling know something we don't?

"Avram Grant literally is in a no-win situation
- unless he wins."

**Graham Taylor offers hope to the
Chelsea boss**

"He had it on a plate, he had the sausage,
bacon and eggs on it as well, but he
couldn't take it."

**Chris Kamara makes a meal of his
breakfast analogy**

"Today will live with them for the rest of their
lives. Well, at least through the summer."

**Jamie Redknapp dramatically shortens
footballers' life expectancy**

"Arsene Wenger uses the FA Cup to bleed his youngsters."

It's tough being an Arsenal youngster, according to Alvin Martin

"Diouf is a master of the dark art of the winger. He draws you in, then he sucks you off."

Garry Birtles appears to be on intimate terms with El-Hadji Diouf

"Of course, Steven Gerrard is one of only a few Liverpool players who never gets left out by Rafa. And even he doesn't always get picked."

David Pleat reflects on Benitez's rotation policy

"Man United's defensive record is second to none... apart from Liverpool's that is."

Warren Barton gets his back fours confused

"Late goals come in short bursts and Sunderland's burst has gone on for a long time."

Phil Thompson on the Black Cats' staying power

"David Moyes does like to get dirty with his players."

Team bonding at Everton, according to Charlie Nicholas

"Today I'm joined by Paul Walsh who won the
Cup with Spurs in 1991, Phil Thompson who won
it in 1974, Paul Merson who won it in 1993 and
Matt Le Tissier. What are you doing here?"
Jeff Stelling puts the boot in on
Soccer Saturday

"Parkin's making a run towards the box,
he might get there sometime this week."
Jonathan Pearce doesn't rate Jon
Parkin's pace then

"A memorable half hour to forget!"
Alan McInally is in two minds about
the first 30 minutes

"They are fourth in the Championship, and you can't ask for more than that."

Mark Bright aims low

"We all thought West Ham were dead and buried when they lost 4-3 to West Ham."

Jamie Redknapp on a very local derby

"If you keep walking past the barbers, eventually you'll get a haircut."

Paul Merson muses on Middlesbrough's relegation prospects

"Marseille needed to score first and that never looked likely once Liverpool had taken the lead."

Nothing gets past David Pleat

"Scholes walks away a bit gingerly."

David Pleat states the insultingly obvious

"I understand why Paul Jewell took the Derby job, but I just wonder why he went there."

Phil Thompson was thinking of the "other" Derby job

"I'm not saying we shouldn't have a foreign manager, but I think he should definitely be English."

Paul Merson wants an Anglo-English England manager

"Diouf's got more previous than
Jack the Ripper."
**Colin Murray pays the Bolton
striker the ultimate compliment**

"Liverpool were all mishy-mashy. I know that
isn't a word, but it should be."
Paul Merson, a modern-day Doctor Johnson

"Michael Dawson clearly put his ball
to the hand."
What game is Iain Dowie watching?

"If United don't equalise, they might
lose this game."
Micky Thomas cuts to the chase

"They'll have to literally have eyes

in the back of their heads."

Jamie Redknapp wants mutant players

"Theo Walcott is carrying a nation,

literally, on his shoulders."

Andy Townsend reckons Walcott is

some sort of Charles Atlas

"Arsene would've thought in the past,

'Thierry will get me 20, Pires 15,

Ljungberg 12.' That's 50 goals."

George Graham failed GCSE maths

SAY WHAT?

"Anelka used to have days where he'd seem to have got up on the wrong side of the bed. Maybe Sam's pushed it up against the wall so he can only get out on the good side."

Paul Merson lifts the lid on Sam Allardyce's innovative management techniques

"And here's Jose Mourinho talking to the Chelsea manager Garth Crooks."

Stamford Bridge role reversal courtesy of 5 Live's Spoony

"What will you do when you leave football, Jack – will you stay in football?"

Stuart Hall, broadcasting genius

"If you keep walking past the barbers, eventually you'll get a haircut."

Paul Merson on avoiding relegation

"Nobody is Didier Drogba."

Phil Thompson on Chelsea's non-existent striker

"If Malbranque's early chance had gone in, we'd have a completely different scoreline."

Alan Green is definitely keeping count

"Ashley Cole is getting a good deal of stick - but then you'd expect that when you're playing away from home."

Match of the Day's Steve Wilson

"Alan McInally never broke a metatarsal
in his career. Matt Le Tissier never
broke sweat in his."
Jeff Stelling sticks the boot in again

"He's ike 6ft 4in of blancmange...
more Swiss Toni than Luca Toni."
**Mark Lawrenson on the off-form
Italian striker**

"Is the way Rooney and Tevez play off
the cuff or just as it happens?"
Geoff Shreeves answers his own question

"Arsene Wenger built a stadium at Arsenal,
though he didn't actually build a stadium."
Tony Gale is the architect of his own downfall

"David Unsworth is fatter than me and
Gavin Mahon couldn't even pass wind
accurately today."
**Commentator Martin Price is thrilled
with his visit to Vicarage Road**

"Steven Gerrard was Liverpool's only senior
player tonight. Well, OK, they had two: Hyypia,
Gerrard, Fowler and Dudek. So that's four."
Jamie Redknapp gets there in the end

"I'd compare him to the incomparable
George Best."

**David Pleat on the one and only
Cristiano Ronaldo**

"We want zero-tolerance on players sliding in,
but sometimes you have to let one or two go."

Chris Kamara is prepared to bend the rules

"If they released a Titus Bramble bloopers
DVD, it would be four hours long."

Adrian Chiles twists the knife

"He looks like a fish up a tree
- out of his depth."

Confusion reigns for Paul Merson

"Ballack is having a nightmare.

They'll be changing his name soon."

Chris Waddle, cunning linguist

"The opening ceremony was good,

although I missed it."

You've got to admire Graeme

Le Saux's honesty

"There's one that hasn't been cancelled

because of the Arctic conditions –

it's been cancelled because of a frozen pitch."

Bob Wilson

"It's end-to-end stuff, all at one end."

Jeff Stelling

"In the bottom nine positions of the league there are nine teams."
Ray Stubbs

"Arsenal could have got away with a nil-nil, if it wasn't for the two goals."
Des Lynam

"Despite the rain, it's still raining here at Old Trafford."
Jimmy Hill

"There were two Second Division matches last night, both in the Second Division."
Dominic Allen

"Peter Shilton conceded five, and you

don't get many of those to the dozen."

Des Lynam

"Chesterfield 1 Chester 1 - another

score draw in the local derby."

Des Lynam

"It's a renaissance, or put more simply,

some you win, some you lose."

Des Lynam

"Manchester United are looking to Frank

Stapleton to pull some magic out of the fire."

Jimmy Hill

"In Scotland football hooliganism has been met by banning alcohol from grounds but in England this solution has been circumnavigated."

Wallace Mercer

"Kicked wide of the goal with such precision."

Des Lynam

"When I'm out on the pitch it's the closest thing to being back in a dressing room."

Steve Baines

"David [Johnson] has scored 62 goals in 148 games for Ipswich and those statistics tell me that he plays games and scores goals."
David Platt

"Our talking point this morning is George Best, his liver transplant and the booze culture in football. Don't forget, the best caller wins a crate of John Smith's."
Alan Brazil

"Don't hoover up while Chelsea are playing because if you knock the telly, Robben will fall over."
Ruud Gullit thinks Robben is a soft touch

"Terrible marking, you don't mark open spaces. Open space has never scored a goal in a football match."

Steve McMahon isn't impressed with the defence

"Everton have not won without being in the lead."

Andy Gray sums up the Merseyside derby

"It's not easy on the eye but it's super to watch."

Steve Claridge has double vision

"Matt Taylor is off - and what a chance he had. Two chances - three in fact, actually, if you count the third."

Gary Weaver can't make his mind up

"Steven Reid's knee has blown up, so we've sent him back to Blackburn."

Ray Houghton reflects on an explosive tackle

"Milan Baros isn't the greatest-looking of players."

Jamie "Handsome" Redknapp doesn't fancy Villa's striker

"Fuller scored Stoke's penalty, putting it in the wrong corner."

There's just no pleasing John Solako...

"When you get injured at 20, it's not a problem because you're fit."

Phil Thompson fails to grasp the concept of "injured"

"When you concede two goals, you've got to score three to win a game."

Peter Reid's sums are impeccable

"The defender was so laid back there he was almost vertical."

Frank Stapleton loses his bearings

"They have to concentrate not only when they have the ball or when their opponents have the ball, but also when neither of them has the bal**l.**"

Graham Taylor covers all the bases

"I used to think my name was 'Stop The Cross', I heard it so much."

Lee Dixon has an identity crisis

"Ian Pearce has limped off with what looks like a shoulder injury."

Tony Cottee failed his medical exams

"When you're walking onto a bus and trying
to get there before the person in front of you,
that's a different level of competition to playing
in front of 80,000 people."
**Graeme Le Saux never gets a seat
on the 8:15**

"I was inbred into the game by my father."
David Pleat reveals a disturbing family secret

"Last year's race was a bit of a damp squid."
Mark Hateley

"It was that game that put the Everton ship
back on the road."
Alan Green, all at sea

"Tugay is writhing all over the place

as if he were dead."

Alan Green has been watching

too many zombie films

"A tremendous free kick. It probably

would have gone in if he had put it

where he intended to put it."

Stan Collymore's a stickler for accuracy

"I was saying the other day how often

the most vulnerable area for goalies is

between their legs."

Andy Gray, anatomy expert

"For such a small man Maradona gets great elevation on his balls."

David Pleat

"Ghana are finding it difficult to impregnate the Cameroon defence."

A Eurosport commentator who may have meant to use the word "penetrate" instead

"Jean Tigana has spent the entire first half inside Liam Brady's shorts."

Jimmy Magee

"It looks like he's got a bit of a knock there,

judging by the language on his face."

The player's face speaks volumes,

according to Clive Tyldsley

"Nervy, edgy, cautious – a bit like

Alan Hansen on the dancefloor."

Gary Lineker puts the boot in

"They say football is unscripted drama

and this match certainly hasn't followed

the script tonight."

Conor McNamara loses the plot

"In the bottom nine positions of the league there are nine teams."

Ray Stubbs' sums are impeccable

"Chris Porter scored his first league goal last week, and he's done the same this week."

Jeff Stelling experiences a strong sense of déjà vu

"Matt Taylor is off - and what a chance he had. Two chances - three in fact, if you count the third."

Gary Weaver on Bolton-Portsmouth

"Football's football. If that weren't the case, it wouldn't be the game that it is."
It's hard to argue with Garth Crooks

"It's one of the greatest goals ever, but I'm surprised that people are talking about it being the goal of the season."
Andy Gray can't quite make his mind up

"The one thing Cristiano Ronaldo has is pace, quick feet and an eye for goal."
That's three things, Chris Waddle

"The club has literally exploded."
Ian Wright gets a tad carried away

"The penalty was as clear as night is day."

Alan Green doesn't know what time it is

"It was against Chelsea that Peter Crouch had that giraffe-on-acid moment."

Jeff Stelling let his imagination run wild

"Nicolas Anelka is so physically strong, he's not unlike Anelka."

Jamie Redknapp thinks the French striker has a twin

"When you're down, you Palace fans, the fickle finger of fate rarely smiles on you."

Jonathan Pearce mixes his metaphors

"You've got to take the rough with the smooth. It's like love and hate, war and peace, all that bollocks."
Ian "Mr Sensitive" Wright

"You talk about captaincy and leadership, that's no captaincy. He's acting like it's the last day of the season and they've lost the title. I played for managers that would be turning in their graves. He's the captain!"
Alan Hansen disapproves of William Gallas's histrionic reaction to Arsenal's 2-2 draw away to Birmingham City

"It's end-to-end stuff, but from side to side."

Trevor Brooking

"Julian Dicks is everywhere. It's like they've got 11 Dicks on the field."

Metro Radio

"Gareth Jellyman of Mansfield Town has been sent off, hope he doesn't throw a wobbly."

Jeff Stelling

"I think this could be our best victory over Germany since the war."

John Motson loses all perspective

"The lad got overexcited when he saw the whites of the goalpost's eyes."

Steve Coppell

"He's pulling him off! The Spanish manager is pulling his captain off."

Irish commentator George Hamilton

"He's passing the ball like Idi Amin."

Alan Parry

"Argentina are the second-best team in the world, and there's no higher praise than that."

Ron Atkinson

"Lee Sharpe has got dynamite in his shorts."

Stuart Hall

"If Plan A fails, they could always revert

to Plan A."

Mark Lawrenson doesn't like teams

changing tactics

"This game is, I think, what my children

would describe as 'pants'."

Gary Lineker makes presenting look

like child's play

"Now Zola tries to inject some speed..."

Ron Jones

"That was only a yard away from being an inch-perfect pass."

Murdo MacLeod

"The World Cup is a truly international event."

John Motson

"That's an old Ipswich move – O'Callaghan crossing for Mariner to drive over the bar."

John Motson

"I would not say that he [David Ginola] is one of the best left-wingers in the Premiership, but there are none better."

Ron Atkinson

"He's not only a good player, but he's spiteful in the nicest sense of the word."

Ron Atkinson

"Well, that's not attractive to watch... which leads us rather aptly to Phil Thompson."

Jeff Stelling

"They've picked their heads up off the ground, and they now have a lot to carry on their shoulders."

Ron Atkinson

"If history repeats itself, I should think we can expect the same thing again."

Terry Venables

"It's understandable that people are keeping one eye on the pot and another up the chimney."

Kevin Keegan

"I'd love to be a mole on the wall in the Liverpool dressing room at half-time."

Kevin Keegan

"We managed to wrong a few rights."

Kevin Keegan

"He transfixed the static Liverpool defence like a stoat on the rabbit."

Stuart Hall on Jimmy Floyd Hasselbaink

"That's often the best place to beat a
goalkeeper, isn't it, between the legs?"
Clive Tyldesley

John Motson: "Bramall Lane is a fantastic
place, and I believe one of the only grounds
to host an FA Cup Final and Test Match cricket."
Mark Lawrenson: "Stay in last night did
you, John?"
**Mark Lawrenson implies that co-commentator
John Motson is a bit of a swot**

"When you speak to Barry Fry, it's like
completing a 1,000-piece jigsaw."
Brian Moore

"United are looking to make the Glazers double Glazers."

Clive Tyldesley during the Champions League final

"They've flown in from all over the world, have the rest of the world team."

Brian Moore

"He must be lightning slow."

Ron Atkinson

"He'll take some pleasure from that, Brian Carey. He and Steve Bull have been having it off all afternoon."

Ron Atkinson

"There's lots of balls dropping off people."

Ron Atkinson

"The winners [of the Champions League] stand to make £10 million in prize money – that's before any money they can make on programme sales, hot dogs and the like."

Brian Moore

"Cantona's is speaking the whole French dictionary without saying a word."

Barry Davies

"The Dutch look like a huge jar of marmalade."

Barry Davies

"If Glenn Hoddle said one word to his team at half-time, it was concentration and focus."

Ron Atkinson commentating on England-Argentina in 1998

"Glenn Hoddle hasn't been the Hoddle we know. Neither has Bryan Robson."

Ron Greenwood

"If ever the Greeks needed a Trojan horse, it is now."

Gerald Sinstadt

"And now we have the formalities over, we'll have the national anthems."

Brian Moore

"The only thing Norwich didn't get was the goal they finally got."

A tongue-tied Jimmy Greaves

"He chanced his arm with his left foot."

Trevor Brooking

"Nicolas Anelka left Arsenal for £23 million and they built a training ground on him."

Kevin Keegan on what happens to Arsenal players who stray

"It's headed away by John Clark, using his head."

Derek Rae

"Welcome to Bologna on Capital Gold for England versus San Marino with Tennent's Pilsner, brewed with Czechoslovakian yeast for that extra Pilsner taste and England are one down."

Jonathan Pearce gets his priorities right

"Arsenal are quick to credit Bergkamp with laying on 75 per cent of their nine goals."

Tony Gubba does the maths

"Tottenham are trying tonight to become the first London team to win this cup. The last team to do so was the 1973 Spurs team."

Mike Ingham

"...so different from the scenes in 1872, at the cup final none of us can remember."

John Motson

"Well that was much Adu about nothing really."

Mark Lawrenson on a botched free kick by Freddy Adu

"For those of you watching in black and white, Spurs are in the yellow strip."

John Motson

"And Seaman, just like a falling oak, manages to change direction."

John Motson

"It was the game that put the Everton ship back on the road."
Alan Green

"The Uruguayans are losing no time in making a meal around the referee."
Mike Ingham

"He's 31 this year: last year he was 30."
David Coleman

"One or two of their players aren't getting any younger."
Clive Tyldesley

"You might say that Frings can only get better..."

You said it, Andy Gray, about Torsten Fring's broken rib

"Madrid are like a rabbit dazed in the headlights of a car, except this rabbit has a suit of armour, in the shape of two precious away goals."

George Hamilton

"I'm sure coach Frank Rijkaard will want the Dutch to go on and score a fourth now – although obviously they'll have to score the third one first."

Angus 'Statto" Loughran

"There'll be no siestas in Madrid tonight."

Kevin Keegan

"I came to Nantes two years ago and it's much the same today, except that it's completely different."

Kevin Keegan

"In some ways, cramp is worse than having a broken leg."

Kevin Keegan

"He's showed him the left leg, then the right. Where's the ball, the defender asks? It's up his sleeve."

Clive Tyldesley

"Ziege hits it high for Heskey,

who isn't playing."

Alan Green

"Ardiles strokes the ball like it was a part of his

anatomy."

Jimmy Magee

"Well, Clive, it's all about the two Ms

- movement and positioning."

Ron Atkinson

"Xavier, who looks just like Zeus,

not that I have any idea what Zeus looks like..."

Alan Green

"They [Bayern Munich] lost in the semi-finals of the Champions League to Real Madrid last year, and the year before that were beaten in the final by Manchester United, so their European pedigree is second to none."

Simon Brotherton

"David O'Leary's poker face betrays the emotions."

Clive Tyldesley

"Their strength is their strength."

Ron Atkinson

"Jari Litmanen should be made compulsory."

Ron Atkinson

"The ball goes down the keeper's throat where it hits him on the knees to say the least."

Ron Atkinson

"We haven't had a strategic free kick all night. No one's knocked over attackers ad lib."

Ron Atkinson

"It slid away from his left boot, which was poised with the trigger cocked."

Barry Davies

"A win tonight is the minimum City

must achieve."

Alan Parry

"He had an eternity to play that ball,

but he took too long over it."

Martin Tyler

"Ritchie has now scored 11 goals, exactly double

the number he scored last season."

Alan Parry

"Wigan Athletic are certain to be promoted

barring a mathematical tragedy."

Tony Gubba

"Welcome to the Nou Camp stadium in Barcelona, which is packed to capacity ... with some patches of seats left empty."

George Hamilton

"John Arne Riise was deservedly blown up for that foul."

Alan Green

"It flew towards the roof of the net like a Wurlitzer."

George Hamilton

"The Everton fans are massed in the Station End, and Lee Carsley is attacking those fans now."

John Murray

"He is the man who has been brought
on to replace Pavel Nedved. The
irreplaceable Pavel Nedved."
Clive Tyldesley

"He's not George Best, but then again,
no one is."
Clive Tyldesley

"The ageless Teddy Sheringham, 37 now..."
Tony Gubba

"Hagi has got a left foot like Brian Lara's bat."
Don Howe

"Hagi could open a tin of beans with his left foot."

Ray Clemence

"I'd say he's the best in Europe, if you put me on the fence."

Sir Bobby Robson

"The atmosphere here is literally electric."

John Motson

"And what a time to score! Twenty-two minutes gone."

John Motson

"Brazil – they're so good it's like they are running around the pitch playing with themselves."
John Motson

"Glenn is putting his head in the frying pan."
Ossie Ardiles

"England now have three fresh men, with three fresh legs."
Jimmy Hill

"Unfortunately, we don't get a second chance. We've already played them twice."
Trevor Brooking

"Stoichkov is pointing at the bench
with his eyes."

David Pleat

"I think it's that lack of width with his height."

Trevor Brooking

"The Arsenal defence is skating close
to the wind."

Jack Charlton

"Brazil, the favourites – if they are the
favourites, which they are..."

Brian Clough

"They've missed so many chances they must be wringing their heads in shame."

Ron Greenwood

"Merseyside derbies usually last 90 minutes and I'm sure today's won't be any different."

Trevor Brooking

"Scoles is now on his feet in front of us, but very gingerly."

Clive Tyldesley

"Football's football: if that weren't the case it wouldn't be the game that it is."

Garth Crooks

"And there's Ray Clemence looking as cool as ever out in the cold."

Jimmy Hill

"He's got a brain under his hair."

David Pleat

"If there are any managers out there with a bottomless pit, I'm sure that they would be interested in these two Russians."

David Pleat

Jimmy Hill "Don't sit on the fence Terry, what chance do you think Germany has got of getting through?"

Terry Venables "I think it's fifty-fifty."

"He hit the post, and after the game
people are going to say, well, he hit the post."
Jimmy Greaves

"He held his head in his hands as it
flashed past the post."
Alan Brazil

"It's like a big Christmas pudding out there."
Don Howe

"Venison and Butcher are as brave as
two peas in a pod."
John Sillett

"He was as game as a pebble."

David Webb

"Most of the players will be wearing

rubbers tonight."

Gary Lineker

"They've come out with all cylinders flying."

Luther Blissett

"Germany are probably, arguably,

undisputed champions of Europe."

Bryan Hamilton

"Fiorentina start the second half attacking their fans; just the way they like things."

Ray Wilkins

"In the words of the old song, it's a long time from May to December but, you know, it's an equally long time from December to May."

Jimmy Hill

"Like Jim Smith's [Derby] side this year, we were answering our own questions."

Kevin Hector

"Apart from their goals, Norway wouldn't have scored."

Terry Venables

"Manchester United have hit the ground running - albeit with a 3-0 defeat."

Bob Wilson

"That's no remedy for success."

Chris Waddle

"The World Cup is every four years, so it's going to be a perennial problem."

Gary Lineker

"He's not going to adhere himself to the fans."

Alan Mullery

"It's sometimes easier to defend a one-goal
lead than a two-goal lead."

Mark Lawrenson

"Batistuta gets most of his goals with the ball."

Ian St John

"There won't be a dry house in the place."

Mark Lawrenson

"The candle is still very much in
the melting pot."

Alan McInally

"All the cul-de-sacs are closed for Scotland."

Joe Jordan

"Hearts are now playing with a five-man back four."

Alan McInally

"The club has literally exploded."

Ian Wright

"He's like all great players – he's not a great player yet."

Trevor Francis

"Historically, the host nations do well in Euro 2000."

Trevor Brooking

"If Glenn Hoddle had been any other nationality, he would have had 70 or 80 caps for England."

John Barnes

"Kevin Keegan said if he had a blank sheet of paper, five names would be on it."

Alvin Martin

"He's a two-legged tripod, if you know what I mean."

Graham Richards

"He was just about to pull the trigger on his left foot."

Terry Butcher

"You either win or you lose. There's no in between."

Terry Venables

"[Like] a woman on her wedding day - nervous, out of position and hoping everything would soon be over so she could go up to the bedroom."

Hugo Gatti in Spanish newspaper *Marca*

"He's looking around at himself."

Jimmy Greaves

"Roy Keane, his face punches the air..."

Alan Brazil

"They are conceding more goals than you would expect them to and they are letting them in at the other end."

Ray Clemence emphasizes his point

"Those are the sort of doors that get opened if you don't close them."

Terry Venables

"And for those of you watching without television sets, live commentary is on Radio 2."

David Coleman

"Chris Waddle is off the pitch at the moment - exactly the position he is at his most menacing."

Gerald Sinstadt

"If they play together, you've got two of them."

Dion Dublin

"Two-nil was a dangerous lead to have..."

Peter Beardsley

"The one thing England have got is spirit, resolve, grit and determination."

Alan Hansen

"He hasn't been the normal Paul Scholes today, and he's not the only one."

Alvin Martin

"He hits it into the corner of the net as straight as a nut."

David Pleat

"That was an inch-perfect pass to no one."

Ray Wilkins

"There's Thierry Henry, exploding like the French train that he is."

David Pleat

"He's got two great feet. Left foot, right foot, either side."

Alan Hansen

"I don't think anyone enjoyed it. Apart from the people who watched it."

Alan Hansen

"This is a real cat and carrot situation."

David Pleat

"He's got a great future ahead. He's missed so much of it."

Terry Venables

"Not only has he shown Junior Lewis the red card, but he's sent him off."

Chris Kamara

"These managers all know their onions and cut their cloth accordingly."

Mark Lawrenson

"Tempo, now there's a big word."

Barry Venison

"Let's close our eyes and see what happens."

Jimmy Greaves

"Craig Bellamy has literally been on fire."

Ally McCoist

"I think Charlie George was one of Arsenal's all time great players. A lot of people might not agree with that, but I personally do."

Jimmy Greaves

"Ian Rush unleashed his left foot and it hit the back of the net."

Mike England

"He's perfectly fit, apart from his physical fitness."

Mike England

"That's bread and butter straight down the goalkeeper's throat."

Andy Gray

"Roy Evans bleeds red blood."

Alan Mullery

"Every time they attacked we were memorized by them."

Charlie Nicholas

"It's a tense time for managers. They have to exhume confidence."

Gary Lineker

"He looks as though he's been playing for England all his international career."

Trevor Brooking

"You could visibly hear the strain in his voice."

Mike Parry

"The Belgians will play like their fellow

Scandinavians, Denmark and Sweden."

Andy Townsend

"Michael Owen is not a diver. He knows when to

dive, and when not to."

Steve Hodge

"The atmosphere here is thick and fast."

Chris Kamara

"The first two-syllable word I learned when I was growing up was 'discretion'."
Eamon Dunphy

"I watched the game, and I saw an awful lot of it."
Andy Gray

"Gary Neville was palpable for the second goal."
Mark Lawrenson

"PSV have got a lot of pace up front. They're capable of exposing themselves."
Barry Venison

"He's got a knock on his shin there, just above the knee."

Frank Stapleton

"There will be a game where somebody scores more than Brazil and that might be the game that they lose."

Sir Bobby Robson

"Solskjaer never misses the target. That time he hit the post."

Peter Schmeichel

"At the end of the day, the team with the most points are champions, apart from when it goes to goal difference."
Tony Cottee

"Now they have got an extra yard of doubtness in their minds."
Chris Kamara

"He's good at that, David Beckham. He's good at kicking the ball."
Jimmy Armfield

"He is like an English equivalent of Teddy Sheringham."
Trevor Brooking

"It's his outstanding pace that stands out."

Robbie Earle

"Spurs did well in the first half, closing

Tottenham down."

Spurs man-marked themselves,

according Robbie Earle

"The fact that Burnley got beat here already

will stick in their claw."

Mark Lawrenson

"Wayne Rooney really has a man's body

on a teenager's head."

George Graham

"He went down like a pack of cards."

Chris Kamara

"Peter Beardsley has got a few tricks

up his book."

Ian Snodin

"He signals to the bench with his groin."

Mark Bright

"I saw him kick the bucket over there, which

suggests he's not going to be able to continue."

Trevor Brooking

"They've forced them into a lot of unforced errors."
Steve Claridge

"You takes your money, you pays your choice, sort of thing."
Tim Flowers

"The one thing Gordon has brought to this team is a bit of work-rate and team spirit."
Robbie Earle

"If you had a linesman on each side of the pitch in both halves you'd have nearly four."
Robbie Earle

"The goal that Charlton scored has aroused Arsenal."

George Graham

"The managerial vacancy at the club remains vacant."

Trevor Brooking

"Bridge has done nothing wrong, but his movement's not great and his distribution's been poor."

Alan Mullery

"I was in Moldova airport and I went into the duty-free shop - and there wasn't a duty-free shop."

Andy Gray

"And now for international soccer special: Manchester United versus Southampton."

David Coleman

"More football later, but first let's see the goals from the Scottish Cup final."

Des Lynam

"And now the goals from Carrow Road, where the game finished nil-nil."

Elton Welsby

"This would cut hooliganism in half by 75 per cent."
Tommy Docherty

"If you were in the Brondby dressing room right now, which of the Liverpool players would you be looking at?"
Ray Stubbs

"He [Stan Mortensen] had a cup final named after him: the Matthews Final."
Lawrie McMenemy

"The match will be shown on Match of the Day this evening. If you don't want to know the result, look away now as we show you Tony Adams lifting the trophy for Arsenal."
Steve Rider

"We have more non-English players in our league than any other country in the world."
Gordon Taylor

"Football today would certainly not be the same if it had not existed."
Elton Welsby

"Their team is like a bad haircut,

long up front but short at the back."

Robbie Earle

"We respect them for the good players that they are, but at the end of the day if you have to kick them, you kick them."

Scotland striker Kenny Miller

Chapter Six:
THE GLOBAL GAME

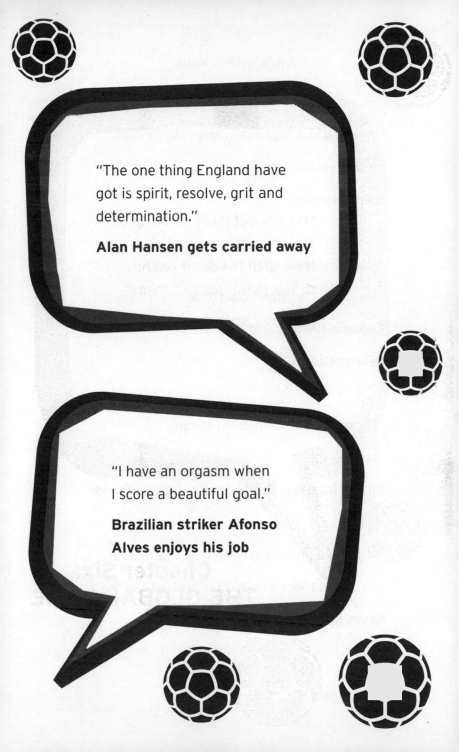

"International football is one clog further up the football ladder."

Glenn Hoddle

"After six weeks in the England camp, even Jack Charlton could look attractive."

England 1966 World Cup winner

George Cohen

"There is great harmonium in the dressing room."

Sir Alf Ramsey on his musical England side

"Argentina are the second best team in the world, and there's no higher praise than that."

Kevin Keegan puts his foot in it

"We were in an awkward position against Yugoslavia, in that in order to win we needed to score more goals then they did."
Spanish coach Jose Antonio Camacho feels sorry for himself

"The Belgian team were just standing around looking at each other, and that's no remedy for success."
Chris Waddle teaches English as a second language

"Francesco Totti and Alessandro Nesta
are like two children pulling a sickie,
pretending they have tummy aches to
avoid sitting a test in class."

**Italy boss Roberto Donadoni isn't
convinced his stars are injured**

"To leave Madrid is to take a step
backwards, or to the side, but it's almost
never a step forward."

Gary Lineker can't decide which way to go

"When you score goals you are great.
When you don't, you are fat."

Ronaldo definitely isn't bitter

"I was going to score an own goal, just to say I'd got a hat-trick at Wembley. Then Denis Law, who had played in the 9-3 game, told me that he would kill me if I did that."
Jim Baxter, who scored both of Scotland's goals in a 2-0 win over England in 1962

"If he had said anything to me after the game I would have punched him."
Andy Goram on Paul Gascoigne's goal in the "Auld Enemy" game during Euro 96

"Everybody says Steve McManaman played on the left for me in Euro 96 but he never played on the left. The one time he did play on the left was against Switzerland."

Terry Venables

"I'm nervous about meeting so many new people. It's like when you go out with a woman for the first time – you're bound to wonder how it will end up."

Sven-Göran Eriksson before his first England game in 2001

"Germany are a very difficult team to play ... they had 11 internationals out there today."

Northern Ireland's Steve Lomas

"I want more from David Beckham.
I want him to improve on perfection."
Kevin Keegan

"We've got a monster around our neck after
beating England, but we must feed it."
Australia's Frank Farina

"Playing with wingers is more effective
against European sides like Brazil than
English sides like Wales."
Ron Greenwood

"A little bit the hand of God, a little the head of Diego."
Diego Maradona describing his first goal against England at the 1986 World Cup

"It wasn't the hand of God. It was the hand of a rascal. God had nothing to do with it."
England manager Sir Bobby Robson rejects the notion of divine intervention in Maradona's goal

"Malvinas 2 England 1! We blasted the English pirates with Maradona and a little hand. He who robs a thief has a thousand years of pardon."
Argentinian newspaper *Cronica* in 1986

"I knew my England career was not going to get off the mark again when manager Graham Taylor kept calling me Tony. That's my dad's name."

Mark Hateley

"Because of the booking I will miss the Holland game – if selected."

Paul Gascoigne

"The little lad jumped like a salmon and tackled like a ferret."

Sir Bobby Robson on Paul Parker's performances at the 1990 World Cup

"We didn't underestimate them. They were a lot better than we thought."
Sir Bobby Robson on England's 1990 World Cup opponents, Cameroon

"Eighteen months ago they [Sweden] were arguably one of the best three teams in Europe, and that would include Germany, Holland, Russia and anybody else if you like."
Sir Bobby Robson

"Everywhere I went people would shout at me, 'What time is it, Frank? Nine past Haffey.'"
Frank Haffey, Scotland's goalkeeper in the same game

"At the time it was really special, especially against the old enemy. In Scotland they try to erase the game from the memory; if you tried to talk about it they'd change the subject."

Jimmy Armfield on England's 9-3 victory over Scotland in 1961

"As we came round the corner from the 18th green, a crowd of members were at the clubhouse window, cheering and waiting to tell me that England had won the World Cup. It was the blackest day of my life."

Scotland striker Denis Law

"The one thing England have got is spirit, resolve, grit and determination."

Alan Hansen gets carried away

"I've never eaten anyone so there is no reason anyone should be scared of me."

Fabio Capello definitely isn't Hannibal Lecter

"You'll have to get on your knees and beg before I play for you again."

Nicolas Anelka wants France boss
Jacques Santini to say sorry

"I strongly feel that the only difference between the two teams were the goals that England scored."
Craig Brown

"We owe the English big time. They stole our land, our oil, perpetrated the Highland Clearances and now they've even pinched Billy Connolly."
Gordon Strachan before the Euro 2000 play-off between England and Scotland

"We have faced African teams, we have faced English teams - so we are ready to face Scotland because we know what their play will be like."

Brazil's Mario Zagallo

"As I was heading towards goal, Alan Ball was shouting: 'Hursty, Hursty give me the ball!' I said to myself: 'Sod you Bally, I'm on a hat-trick.'"

Geoff Hurst recalling his memorable third goal in the 1966 World Cup final

"Russia are a little bit invincible."

Glenn Hoddle is a little bit wrong

"England should've won against Croatia because they had 800 million people in the stadium."
Sky's Alan McInally reflects on a world-record attendance for an international match

"We respect them for the good players that they are but at the end of the day if you have to kick them, you kick them."
Kenny Miller reveals Scotland's no-nonsense tactics

"The England job is an impossible job. Particularly for an Englishman, it's tougher than being Prime Minister."

Glenn Hoddle, who knows a thing or two about the FA hot seat

"He looked like a pint of Guinness running around in the second half."

Paul Gascoigne's description of Paul Ince wearing a head bandage in a crucial match against Italy

"Shearer could be at 100 per cent fitness, but not peak fitness."

Graham Taylor

"What chance has any other top striker got with England while old golden boy Shearer is still on the scene? It's an issue which bugs me."
Andy Cole

"Swedes 2, Turnips 1"
Headline in *The Sun* after England lost to Sweden in 1992

"I used to quite like turnips. Now my wife refuses to serve them."
Graham Taylor

"England have the best fans in the world and Scotland's fans are second-to-none."
Kevin Keegan

"The 33- or 34-year-olds will be 36 or 37 by the time the next World Cup comes around, if they're not careful."

Kevin Keegan identifies a problem for international footballers

"I'm the man for the job. I can revive our World Cup hopes. I couldn't do a worse job, could I?"

Monster Raving Loony Party leader Screaming Lord Sutch puts his name in the frame for the England manager's job in 1994

"Guus Hiddink is lucky. He has a horseshoe as big as my house."

Ruud Gullit on Australia's "fortunate" coach

"I think I'd be brilliant! My ego thinks I'd be brilliant. Actually the rest of me thinks I'd do it brilliantly!"
Martin O'Neill reckons he could do the England job

"Don Revie's decision doesn't surprise me in the slightest. Now I only hope he can quickly learn how to call out bingo numbers in Arabic."
Football League secretary Alan Hardaker after Revie, who was famous for organizing his players' leisure time, left the England job to manage in the UAE

"I have to be honest and say that I felt Sir Bobby Robson was a bit bumbling at times. When I first turned up for training, he called me Paul Adams."

Tony Adams in 1998

"'Wait until you come to Turkey' was the shout, with fingers being passed across throats. And that was just the kitman!"

Gareth Southgate on Turkish reaction to an England victory in 2003

"The nice aspect of football captaincy is that the manager gets the blame if things go wrong."

Gary Lineker on being made England captain

"Michael Owen is a goalscorer - not a
natural born one, not yet, that takes time."
Glenn Hoddle speaking at the
1998 World Cup

"If he was chocolate, he would eat himself."
Unidentified England player during
Glenn Hoddle's reign

"I can't say England are sh*te because
they beat us in the [Euro 2000] play-offs,
and that would make us even sh*ttier."
Former Scotland striker Ally McCoist

"The Germans only have one player under 22,
and he's 23."

**Kevin Keegan on England's
Euro 2000 opponents**

"Portugal play football as I like to see it played.
As a neutral it was fantastic. Unfortunately
I'm not a neutral."

**England manager Kevin Keegan after
Portugal beat England at Euro 2000**

"I feel I have broken the ice with the English
people. In 60 days, I have gone from being
Volvo Man to Svensational."

**Sven-Göran Eriksson after his first game
as England manager in 2001**

"At last England have appointed a manager who speaks English better than the players."

Brian Clough reacts to Eriksson's appointment

"I have no doubts whatsoever that Germany will thrash England and qualify easily for the World Cup. What could possibly go wrong? The English haven't beaten us in Munich for a hundred years."

Former Germany player Uli Hoeness before England beat Germany 5-1 in 2001

"We needed Winston Churchill and we got Iain Duncan Smith."

Anonymous England defender on Sven-Göran Eriksson's half-time team-talk during the England-Brazil game in 2002

"We went out with a whimper in the Brazil game. There was no fight. I'd rather you get Martin Keown on and put him up front and go out fighting."

Steve McManaman on England's 2002 World Cup exit

"I wonder what the Italian media will say? They are not accustomed to being nice about me."

Adriano enjoys the press's discomfort

"It was obvious England were overawed by Brazil, Brazil with ten players, men against boys. You could see England's body language at the end: 'We've done OK, haven't we? Got to the quarter-finals.'"

Roy Keane

"It's amazing what you can see through Sven's specs - I must get a pair."

Gary Lineker as Sven-Göran Eriksson attempts to gloss over another limp England performance

"There have, of course, been worse moments in English history - the Roman Conquest, the Black Death, the Civil War, the fall of France in 1940 and virtually the whole of the 1970s, for example."

Leader in *The Times* putting England's 2002 World Cup failure in perspective

"We were encouraged to open ourselves to the Japanese cuisine on offer, but having been away from home for so long I could have died for a McDonald's."

Danny Mills on the England team's World Cup diet in 2002

"The Italians aren't the youngest side and may not be able to keep it up for 90 minutes."
Pat Nevin casts aspersions on AC Milan's stamina

"When an Italian tells me it's pasta on the plate I check under the sauce to make sure."
Alex Ferguson does his bit for Anglo-Italian relations

"Being crowned champions this year is a bit like a birth – the more you wait, the more you worry. Let's hope it's not a caesarean."
Lyon boss Gerard Houllier hopes to avoid surgery

"Against Bayern Munich, Maldini didn't make a tackle. That's fantastic. It's an art."
Alex Ferguson doesn't like defenders who actually tackle, apparently

"Bernard [Mendy] is a Ferrari. Although, with this Ferrari, we are missing a driver!"
Raymond Domenech damns with faint praise

"There is a Chinese proverb that says when business drags on, it's like fish - it stinks."
Lyon president Jean-Michel Aulas likes his seafood fresh

"You don't have to have been a horse
to be a jockey."
**Arrigo Sacchi lifts the lid on the
sport of kings**

"This squad is effectively a child learning to
walk. We stumbled, we will do so again, but
our fans are there to hold us up."
**Claudio Ranieri hopes to have his
Juventus squad up and running soon**

"We are not phenomenons, we are gladiators."
**Osasuna's Savo Milosevic is a Russell
Crowe fan**

"You score goals as a kid. Then you grow up stupid and become a goalkeeper."

Gianluigi Buffon on the goalkeeping fraternity

"He's a Spaniard, who has come from Spain."

Phil Neville has got Mikel Arteta's number

"PSV have got a lot of pace up front. They're capable of exposing themselves."

Barry Venison reckons the Dutch are fast flashers

"I have an orgasm when I score a beautiful goal."

Brazilian striker Afonso Alves enjoys his job

"If I walked on water, my accusers would say it is because I can't swim."
German legend Berti Vogts just can't win

"How could they not know? It's not chewing gum, doping is like making love, you need two to do it – the doctor and the athlete."
Michel Platini is a man of the world

"I feel OK. The only difference is in training you have the press – and they want to come back home and sleep with you."
Thierry Henry enjoys an intimate relationship with the media in Barcelona

"Everything's been really positive and smooth. Apart from, obviously, the season."

David Beckham is determined to remain positive after signing for LA Galaxy

"I'm starting to believe that Real Madrid can win the Champions League. No, actually, I don't think they can."

Jamie Redknapp is in two minds

"I always pray before matches. I don't ask for victories, I ask God to protect me from injuries."

Bayern Munich's Ze Roberto looks for divine intervention

"Football is a permanent orgasm."

Claude Le Roy must be a very tired man

"Once Celtic got their equaliser, they played a sort of anti-football."

Frank Rijkaard is unimpressed by the Bhoys

"I don't drive a Skoda. After the game with Rangers in Bratislava, I missed the team bus and a journalist gave me a lift in his old Skoda. I drive a BMW."

Artmedia's Balazs Borbely definitely doesn't drive a Skoda

"The Dutch look like a huge jar of marmalade!"

Barry Davies sums up a nation

"If you see a player who's too confident, you might put him on the bench. If he's still not focused, you might have to sell him."

Gerard Houllier is not a man to be messed with

"Although I am not a vain person, I believe I am the best."

Ronaldinho isn't short of confidence

"The worst thing about playing Chelsea is having to listen to Mourinho afterwards."

Barcelona defender Edmilson won't be buying a Stamford Bridge season ticket

"Marseille needed to score first and that never looked likely once Liverpool had taken the lead."
David Pleat doesn't rate the French side's chances

"I'm a little uncomfortable talking about appearing on a postage stamp in Finland."
Jari Litmanen has an irrational fear of Post Offices

"Montella was as calm as a cucumber there."
Gary Stevens knows something about cucumbers the rest of us don't

"[Owen] Hargreaves is well advised to keep quiet. Otherwise I will get very angry and that will not be good for him."

Bayern Munich boss Uli Hoeness has ways of keeping his players quiet

"The coach is not an idiot!"

Italian legend Giovanni Trapattoni puts the case for the defence

"Romario punched me in the face from behind. You know what? I deserved it."

Diego Simeone has a guilty conscience

"Rosenborg's season has finished and you can't tell me that doesn't have an impact on the mental of their team."
Glenn Hoddle thinks Rosenborg are mad

"Put a shit hanging from a stick in the middle of this passionate, crazy stadium and there are people who will tell you it's a work of art. It's not, it's a shit hanging from a stick."
Real Madrid legend Jorge Valdano
doesn't rate Anfield

"I am very happy here in Munich playing for the best team in Europe – that is, unless Real Madrid make Bayern an offer for me."
Brazilian defender Lucio hedges his bets

"I carry on playing and scoring because the new guys are rubbish."
Romario refuses to make way for the next generation

"I am not sure exactly why the winter break started in Germany, but I'm sure it has something to do with the weather."
Owen Hargreaves knows his seasons

"The flight of the ball was really amazing. It was far and high and then it just fell low."
Petr Cech witnesses gravity in action as David Silva scores for Valencia

"People in the street tell me to eat less,

but I look in the mirror and I look OK."

Ronaldinho's happy with his figure

"Taking me from behind is something

that is not worthy behaviour of a man."

Inter Milan's Nicolas Burdisso wants

it up front

"I would say that I am having less sex now

that I'm playing in Serie B. There is more to

think about in this division."

Gianluigi Buffon just isn't the mood

"When Spain's national anthem came on TV,
I sat along and played on the piano."
**Real Madrid coach Bernd Schuster
tickles the ivories**

"Real Madrid need only a draw to qualify
for the knockout stages, but a win might
not be good enough."
Jim Rosenthal dashes Madrid's hopes

"I stopped trying to be beautiful and
thought only of being good."
Ruud van Nistelrooy finally sees sense

"Where I was brought up, they say you have to have received a death certificate before you are declared dead."

At least Roberto Donadoni won't be buried alive

"I was in the doping centre and somebody came in and told me I was in the squad. At first, I thought they were taking the piss out of me."

Italy striker Raffaelle Palladino misses the point

"I hate being kicked when I don't have the ball."

Lionel Messi certainly has a point

"Inzaghi had the number nine, so I went for 99 - nothing to do with ice creams."
Ronaldo clears up the confusion

"Sooner or later I will pose naked to end this discussion of my obesity."
Ronaldo threatens to let it all hang out

"Argentina won't be at Euro 2000 because they're from South America."
Kevin Keegan

"We probably got on better with the likes of Holland, Belgium, Norway and Sweden, some of whom are not even European."
Jack Charlton

"There's a slight doubt about only one player, and that's Tony Adams, who definitely won't be playing tomorrow."
Kevin Keegan

"Beckham will be an average cinema actor living in Hollywood."
Real Madrid president Ramon Calderon thinks Goldenballs is changing careers

"You can't shave my head. Winning the title must be celebrated with dignity."
Stuttgart coach Armin Veh doesn't like coiffure celebrations

"I have shaved the hairs of my legs. I put tape around my ankles and it is always a lot of trouble when the hair sticks to the tape. It's much nicer with a massage as well."

Belgian Logan Bailly is a smooth operator

"It is necessary to wear the sandals of humility and not let the win over Manchester United go to our heads."

Vasco Da Gama coach Antonio Lopes favours modest footwear

"At the moment this isn't a group of men, it is a team of little girls."

Palermo president Maurizio Zamparini thinks his side are wimps

"I never think about beating record. I just try to live from Sunday to Sunday."
Luca Toni takes things on a weekly basis

"Over the years, Dida has shown himself to be a very professional and sporting athlete, who even got back up after he was hit by a firework."
AC Milan boss Carlo Ancelotti thinks his keeper is fireproof

"Fiorentina start the second half attacking their fans, just the way they like things."
Ray Wilkins thinks Italian football is getting too violent

"It's better I don't meet the club's officers any more. They don't listen to my suggestions and I'll just get angry and hang them on the wall."
Christian Vieri isn't a man to be messed with

"We can't behave like crocodiles and cry over spilled milk and broken eggs."
Giovanni Trapattoni, reptile expert

"It was very nice to enter the locker room. There was a good feeling in there, and I got a good feeling from Kevin Doyle and Stephen Hunt."
Reading new boy Marek Matejovsky is touched by his special welcome

"I don't have any particular celebration
- a big smile is all you need."

**Tottenham's new striker Dimitar Berbatov
on his plans to become the Premiership's
smiling assassin**

"I came to England with £900. I learned to
like beans on toast pretty quickly."

Watford's American defender Jay DeMerit

"We lost because we didn't win."

Ronaldo is certainly on the ball

"I decided to come to Portsmouth instead of Marseille because I speak English and my French isn't very good."

Portsmouth's record signing Benjani Mwaruwari, master of pragmatism

"He has played for nearly every club in the world. It is absolutely amazing how much money he's moved for. He is, himself, a bank!"

Arsenal boss Arsene Wenger on Nicolas Anelka following his move to Chelsea in January 2008

"We lost because we didn't win."

Ronaldo is certainly on the ball

"To get players to come to Plymouth
I had to be beat them up and drug them."
**Ian Holloway's drastic measures to
sign new players**

"The fact he personally contacted me
and made so much effort to recruit me,
it has seduced me."
**Bacary Sagna is swept off his feet
by Arsene Wenger**

"On a scale of one to 10, how happy
am I? Try 12."
**Andrew Johnson is delighted to seal his
move to Everton from Crystal Palace**

"Sometimes I'd like to have a conversation with a friend in a restaurant without feeling I'm being watched. At this rate I will have to go on holiday to Greenland. But maybe the Eskimos would know me."

Fernando Torres struggles to adapt to life on Merseyside

"When I left Fenerbache, I would have liked to join a big club. That has not been possible."

Nicolas Anelka endears himself to Bolton fans in the summer of 2006

"I have not got accustomed to English life. The food is truly disastrous and it rains all the time."

Patrice Evra just loves life in Manchester

"If you ask me if I'd pay that amount for any player then I'd say no. It's an outrage!"

Luis Figo on his record £37 million transfer from Barcelona to Real Madrid

"We're building a strong squad in a hurry. Half my players are struggling to find hotels, houses, schools for their kids or even the names of their team-mates."

Billy Davies needs to work on team bonding

"The English players speak fast and they talk with an accent. When I'm walking around the streets of London, people speak so fast that I don't know what they are saying."
Chelsea new-boy Michael Ballack struggles with Cockney rhyming slang

"I struggled the first few days with breakfast. Instead of a croissant and cappuccino, I was faced with eggs."
Manchester City's Rolando Bianchi just can't find a bakery

"I'm much better for having lived in a garage."
New Bolton signing Gretar Steinsson explains the mechanics of the deal

"Obviously no one has shown him how to use the kitchen. If you want to have pasta, why don't you make it, son?"
Alan Green on Rolando Bianchi's culinary conundrum

"The negotiations went very well. The people at Portsmouth know that I will not spend my life at the club. I was able to add a clause to my contract. If I shine, if a really big club wants me, I already know that everything will go well."
Lassana Diarra isn't in it for the long haul

"I can see myself staying at Blackburn for the rest of my career - unless I move to another club."
Benni McCarthy arrives at Ewood Park

"He has South American qualities because he comes from South America."

Jose Mourinho welcomes Claudio Pizarro to Stamford Bridge - for all the right reasons

"He says he's a Red, but they all say that when they sign, don't they?"

Steven Gerrard isn't convinced of Craig Bellamy's Anfield credentials

"I want them to be a bit like the Leeds of old - horrible."

Dennis Wise reveals his tactics after landing the Leeds job

"A new club is like having a new girlfriend
- you don't have feelings straight away."

Michael Owen plays hard to get at Newcastle

"I don't feel integrated into English life at all.
We cannot speak English, we don't know the
culture and we are scared of appearing rude.
My two children are in nursery and I didn't
realise we should take a cake for the rest
of the class on their birthday. In China,
we don't do things like that."

**Manchester City defender Sun Jihai
is homesick**

"I'm going to find out what any new player is like, what he likes for breakfast and what he has on his chips."

Ian Holloway is a stickler for details

"When we agreed a deal, the manager said 'Why don't we sign it at your wedding'?"

Dunfermline boss Jim Leishman really wanted to sign Stephen Simmons

"During the actual games, it is as though everybody's brains are switched off."

Chelsea winger Florent Malouda gets to grips with English football

"I like to go fishing and diving in the Mediterranean. You can't really do that in Coventry."

Michael Mifsud knows his geography

"It was a sense of numbness really – how the hell are we out of this World Cup? It even got to the point where there were weird ideas – maybe if we'd had brown rice rather than white."

Rio Ferdinand clutches at straws after England's 2006 World Cup exit

"The Brazilians were South American, but the Ukrainians will be more European."

...but Phil Neville doesn't

"I lament the score. I'm sorry for Colombia and for my country. We dominated the game."
Colombia coach Jorge Luis Pinto after his side's 5-0 defeat to Paraguay

"Football is not played on paper, it is played on a pitch. This game is not mathematics and in football, two plus two very rarely equals four - it's usually three or five."
Trinidad & Tobago coach Leo Beenhakker reveals why so many footballers fail their maths GCSEs

"Romania are more Portuguese than German."
Barry Venison needs a map...

"If you put an 'o' on the end of his name, then he is going to be good, isn't he?"

Paul Jewell isn't convinced Fabio Capello is the right man for England

"The Belgians will play like their fellow Scandinavians, Denmark and Sweden."

Andy Townsend relocates Brussels

"The fans who want to see Messi, Tevez, Saviola and Aguero all together should go out and rent Snow White and the Seven Dwarfs."

Argentina FA boss Julio Grondona likes big players then

"Sven's a lucky man with the ladies. In fact, he's very lucky because, with respect, he's no Brad Pitt."

Martin O'Neill obviously doesn't fancy the former England boss

"The good news for Nigeria is that they're two-nil down very early in the game."

Kevin Keegan is an optimist

"It was nice to get the first session out of the way and get a bit of a feel for each other."

Steven Gerrard on England's tactile training sessions

Before the Malta game, I ate some white chocolate. I probably had too much but maybe, in a strange way, that helped me to score the hat-trick. I should try this before every game to see if it works."

Slovakia's Filip Sebo is a cocoa champion

"I don't think you can blame a player for missing a penalty. I don't think we missed a penalty individually, I think we missed it collectively."

Stuart Pearce defends his Under-21 charges en masse

"For a game played in Cologne, that stunk."

It's the way Mark Lawrenson tells 'em

"My granny could probably have managed Brazil to World Cup success."

Gary Lineker doesn't rate "Big Phil" Scolari

"I've got the passion but no idea of tactics – I'd be like a black Kevin Keegan."

Ian Wright stakes his claim for the England job

"There's more chance of me flying Concorde to the moon blindfolded than there is of you taking Wales to the South African World Cup."

Robbie Savage's word of encouragement for Wales boss John Toshack

"I enjoy playing against the big men and I will just have to get the stepladder out and get on with it."
Wales' James Collins looks forward to marking 6ft 7in Czech Republic striker Jan Koller

"To be the England manager you must win every game, not do anything in your private life and hopefully not earn too much money."
Sven-Goran Eriksson knows a thing or two about international management

"Zidane can decide a game. When the ball goes to his feet it doesn't cry – when it goes to my feet it cries."

Perhaps "Big Phil" Scolari should change his socks

"I watched a bit of the England game then turned over and watched a Victoria Beckham documentary instead."

Steve Coppell isn't impressed with the Three Lions

"Big Kyle is full of energy, he'd chase paper on a windy day."

Billy Hamilton on Northern Ireland's irrepressible Kyle Lafferty

"I would walk back from the United States
to play for England again."
**David Beckham doesn't mind getting
his feet wet**

"It's about putting square pegs into
square holes."
**Steve McClaren sums up his
England philosophy**

"Why do you go for a foreign guy? It is like you
go to war and say 'Now we choose a general
from Portugal or a general from Italy'. Would
that cross your mind? Never."
**Arsene Wenger is perplexed by Fabio
Capello's appointment as England manager**

"This is a young group and sometimes I don't like some of the things I see. Here we are with another five-star hotel, overlooking the sea at Rimini. So if the waves are making too much noise in the evening, just phone down and we will try to move you to a room on the other side."
Wales boss John Toshack thinks his players are a little too pampered

"It was a very professional performance, but the second half was totally unprofessional."
Kevin Radcliffe on a game of two halves for Wales

"Scotland were like a dog with a bone and when they got the bone, they made it count."
Charlie Nicholas admires Scotland's tenacity

"I feel like a man who has given the double of his key to a mate. The guy comes, takes your car, uses it for 10 days and leaves it in the middle of a field without any petrol."
Arsene Wenger on the perils of players going away on international duty

"Sven was top-drawer and I really liked him. He was straight and honest – even if he did look like Mr Burns from The Simpsons."
David James sums up the feelings of a nation

"England do not have a game until February, so why make a decision over a bacon butty at 8.30am?"

Sir Alex Ferguson on the FA's early-morning decision to axe Steve McClaren

"I'm like milk. Once it's gone past its expiry date you can't drink it anymore."

Spain coach Luis Aragones isn't sour

"The England fans have sat and watched for the first half... now they're giving them the clap."

Graham Taylor on the dubious habits of the Three Lions supporters

"This team has some of the best players in England."

David Beckham assesses the strengths of the England team

"There are no easy games in international football, but I'll go as far as to say that this is one of them."

Craig Bellamy tempts fate

"My players travel more than Phileas Fogg in *Around The World In 80 Days*. Javier Mascherano had to play a friendly for Argentina in Australia. That must have been really important."

Rafa Benitez is not a fan of internationals

"We knew at half-time we were only half-way there."

Wales skipper Simon Davies knows exactly how long a match lasts

"It was a funny one. It was one of them ones that either goes in, or goes over the stand – and as I say, it was neither."

Northern Ireland striker Warren Feeney hedges his bets

"You're not just getting international football, you're getting world football."

Kevin Keegan goes global

"I said right at the start I would live and die by results and results haven't gone my way. In that sense we have failed."
Steve McClaren chooses his words carefully

"Watching the Premier League is like Formula One – it's that quick – and then you go to an international game and it's like a game of chess."
Robert Green wants England to get into second gear

"I think it's the worst job in football."
Neil Warnock doesn't want the England job then

"I've always said that Iraq is the Brazil of the Middle East. We have beautiful skill in this country, we have treasures walking on the ground that we must develop, not just below the ground in the form of oil."

Iraqi coach Sadiq al-Wohali thinks his players are priceless

"He didn't play in any of the six away games in the last qualifying group. We have asked him if he could manage a few this time around - we would appreciate it! Now we have got three away friendlies on the run and the bookies in Cardiff have offered me 11-1 that he won't be in any of them."

Wales boss John Toshack wants Jason Koumas to start playing away

"It was good just to see them train, get a feel of them."
George Burley gets tactile with the Scotland squad

"You always lose when your opponents score and you don't."
France coach Raymond Domenech is nobody's fool

"It was much too intellectual for a footballer to have written it. The spelling and punctuation were all correct."
Curtis Davies reveals how he learned of his England call-up

"I am happy for the fans to chant Beckham's name. He is a very good player and I know him well. But those songs don't influence me at all."
Fabio Capello isn't a music fan

"I am not a Messiah."
Fabio Capello plays down expectations

"The Czech Republic are coming from behind in more than one way now."
John Motson's unfortunate double entendre

"I'm not convinced that Scotland will play a typically English game."
Gareth Southgate insults fans north of the border

"I think that France, Germany, Spain, Holland and England will join Brazil in the semi-finals."
Pele fails to grasp that one plus four makes five

"I don't really like the North. It's always raining. It's very cold and I don't like all those little houses."
Frederic Kanoute on why he stuck to London clubs

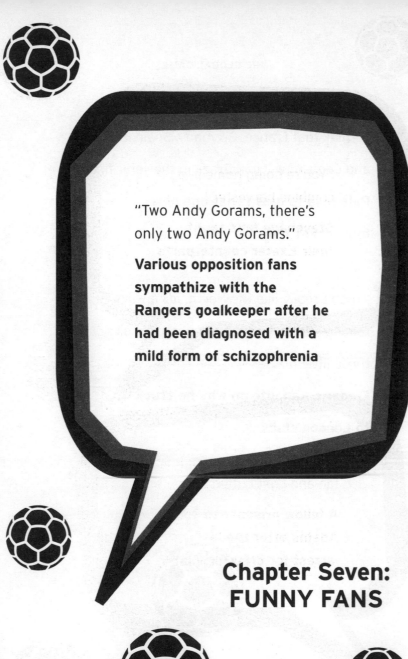

"Two Andy Gorams, there's only two Andy Gorams."

Various opposition fans sympathize with the Rangers goalkeeper after he had been diagnosed with a mild form of schizophrenia

Chapter Seven: FUNNY FANS

"Where's your throw-in gone?"

Heard at Stoke's Britannia Stadium after

Rory Delap was substituted

"You probably think I'm Kenny Samson."

Little Britain's Matt Lucas on meeting

Arsene Wenger who admitted he'd never

seen the show

"We were down at a corner in front of the Kop when they were singing 'You'll Never Walk Alone'. I was standing next to Gerrard and singing along with them. He looked at me like I was a weirdo!"

Havant and Waterlooville's Jamie Collins

lives the dream at Anfield

"If you love Golden Wonder, clap your hands."

Peterborough United fans at Leicester's Walkers' (Crisps) Stadium

"Just one Capello, give him to me, delicious manager, from Italy!"

England fans welcome the new boss

"He's bald, he's old, he never plays in goal – Jens Lehmann, Jens Lehmann."

Arsenal's goalkeeper gets a warm welcome at the City of Manchester Stadium

"You'd better watch out, you'd better not cry,
you'd better watch out, I'm telling you why –
Santa Cruz is coming to Blyth."

**Spartans fans get excited about the arrival
of Blackburn in the FA Cup**

"Tim Timminy, Tim Timminy, Tim Tim Teroo.
We've got Tim Howard and he says f**k you!"

**Everton fans celebrate their Tourettes-
suffering goalkeeper in the style of
Dick Van Dyke**

"We sing better than your wife."

**The DC United crowd let David Beckham
know they're not Spice Girls fans**

"One Lily Savage, there's only one Lily Savage."
Arsenal fans to Blackburn's Robbie Savage

"Mourinho are you listening, you'd better keep our trophy glistening, because we'll be back in May to take it away, walking in a Fergie Wonderland!"
Manchester United fans want the title back at Old Trafford

"We're not fickle. We just don't like you."
Aston Villa supporters get their message across to David O'Leary

"Stevie Gerrard, Gerrard, he kisses the badge on his chest then puts in a transfer request, Stevie Gerrard, Gerrard."

Manchester United supporters question the Liverpool star's loyalty

"He's big, he's Red, his feet hang out his bed, Peter Crouch, Peter Crouch."

Anfield pays homage...

"He's big, he's tall, he's clumsy on the ball – Peter Crouch."

...As do the Everton fans

"He's fat, he's round, he's kicked us out our ground, Robbie Williams, Robbie Williams." **Scotland fans make their feelings clear after the pop star's concert at Hampden forces them to move to Parkhead**

"You're going home in a combine harvester." **Stevenage fans taunt their Exeter counterparts**

"He comes from Zimbabwe, he'll score eventually!" **Portsmouth supporters serenade striker Benjani**

"We hate the English more than you."

Republic of Ireland and Germany fans find something in common

"You're just a fat Spanish waiter."

Bolton fans welcome Liverpool manager Rafa Benitez...

"I remember a big fat red-haired bloke who used to torture us at the start of every season when it was boiling hot. He would lean over the wall with his fat stomach showing and a bottle of beer in his hand and leer at us shouting, 'You're not fit!'"

Francis Lee remembers a particular Manchester City fan

"Complaints, moans, complaints. Now listen to this bit: 'And you can tell Walter Smith to get his finger out of his ar*e.' And ar*e is spelt A–R–S–S."

Rangers chairman David Murray reads out a fan's letter to listening journalists

"Last Thursday we received a letter, dated next Monday, complaining about appalling language in the Shed at today's match against Everton. You have been warned!"

Then Chelsea chairman Ken Bates

"Sit down potato head!"

The West Brom faithful taunt Birmingham boss Steve Bruce

"I can't believe what I've seen tonight. It was a disgrace. If we'd have scored another goal in that atmosphere I don't think we would have got out alive."
Joe Royle after Manchester City's September 1998 visit to Millwall

"It's neat, it's weird, it's Rafa's goatee beard!"
Liverpool supporters reflect on their managers facial hair

"If you made a lot of money selling biscuits, buy our club."
West Ham fans welcome new owner - biscuit baron Eggert Magnusson to tune of a famous biscuit television commercial

"We're gonna deep fry yer tapas!"

Aberdeen fans make themselves

at home in Madrid

"Dichio, Dichio, Danny Dichio, he's got

no hair but we don't care, Danny Dichio!"

Preston fans love their follically-

challenged striker

"There's only one Jimmy Krankie!"

Leeds boss Dennis Wise enjoys a warm

welcome at Molineux

"You're just a fat Eddie Murphy!"

Arsenal fans to Jimmy Floyd Hasselbaink

"One Song, we've only got one Song!"

Charlton supporters salute Alexandre Song

"You only sing when you're fishing!"

Hull City's away support endear

themselves at Grimsby

"One of my most embarrassing confessions

is that I'm a Chelsea fan – but the first time

I ever went to Stamford Bridge was for a

party thrown by Level 42."

 Pop star Nik Kershaw

"He's got no hair, but we don't care,

Martin, Martin, Jol".

Spurs fans salute their Dutch boss

"He's fat, he's round, he bounces all around,

Sammy Lee, Sammy Lee."

The Bolton boss is a firm favourite at Stamford Bridge

"Yousef's here and Yousef's there, here we go,

Moroccan all over the world."

Norwich supporters to Yousef Safri

"Whinge on the telly, he's going to whinge on the telly!"

Middlesbrough fans taunt Bolton boss Sam Allardyce

"He's here, he's there, he wears no underwear,

Lee Bowyer, Lee Bowyer."

Leeds United fans after Bowyer let slip

that he sometimes goes commando

"Fat Eddie Murphy, you're just a fat

Eddie Murphy."

Newcastle United fans take aim at

Jimmy Floyd Hasselbaink

"He's here, he's there, we're not allowed to

swear, Frank Leboeuf, Frank Leboeuf."

Chelsea fans censor themselves after

Leboeuf asked them not to swear when

singing about him

"There's only one Emile Heskey, one Emile Heskey. He used to be sh**e, but now he's all right, Walking in a Heskey wonderland."

Birmingham City fans enjoy their striker's return to form

"Two Andy Gorams, there's only two Andy Gorams."

Various opposition fans sympathize with the Rangers goalkeeper after he had been diagnosed with a mild form of schizophrenia

"If you hate Bryan Robson, throw your shoes!"

Sheffield United fans aren't exactly enamoured by their manager

"Bernt Haas. I've gone and Bernt my Haas.

I've gone and Bernt my Haas. I've gone and

Bernt my Haas. Bernt Haas..."

West Bromwich Albion fans enjoy their

Austrian's player's name

"Whenever I'm in times of trouble, Mother

Mary comes to me, Singing Glasgow Celtic

1, Caley 3. Celtic 1, Caley 3, Celtic 1, Caley 3,

Glasgow Celtic 1, Caley 3."

Rangers fans rejoice in their old rivals'

misfortune to the tune of "Let It Be"

"Beaten by a franchise, you're getting

beaten by a franchise."

MK Dons fans love their history

"If you hate Bryan Robson, throw your shoes!"
Sheffield United fans aren't exactly

enamoured by their manager

"When I first heard the fans chanting, I thought
they were booing me. But I soon understood
what they were saying and that they like me."
Kanu(uuuuuuuu) on the early

days at Arsenal

"Neville Neville, they're in defence, Neville
Neville, their future's immense. Neville
Neville, they ain't half bad, Neville Neville,
it's the name of their dad."
Sung to the tune of David Bowie's

"Rebel Rebel" at Old Trafford

"Don't blame it on the Biscan, Don't blame it on the Hamann, Don't blame it on the Finnan, Blame it on Traore. He just can't, He just can't, He just can't control his feet."
Liverpool fans blame it on the boogie

"Your sister is your mother, your uncle is your brother. You all fu*k one another, the Norwich family."
Visitors to Carrow Road

"What a nightmare. I'm a Tottenham fan and I get cuffed to you."
A fellow prisoner to Tony Adams after the latter's arrest for drink-driving

"I vividly remember a nil-nil with Leeds.
It was one of my all-time favourite matches
- only an Arsenal supporter could say that
of a goalless draw."
Ray Davies of The Kinks

"When we had been there as players, two
bad games and the fans were on your back;
three bad games and they were rocking your
car, trying to turn it over."
Alan Mullery remembers his Spurs days

"Who's the midget in the suit?"
**West Ham fans salute vertically-
challenged Bolton boss Sammy Lee**

"He's big, he's Scouse, he looks like Mickey Mouse – it's Franny Jeffers, Franny Jeffers!"
Sheffield Wednesday fans salute their club's new signing

"You lose some, you draw some."
Comedian Jasper Carrott on being a Birmingham City fan

"We don't welcome yobs in any form, but that isn't to say we're against tribal loyalty. And our tribe aren't half fearsome when they want something."
Karren Brady on Birmingham City's fans

"The club call us hooligans, but who'd cheer them if we didn't come? You have to stand there and take it when Spurs are losing and others are jeering at you. It's not easy. We support them everywhere and get no thanks."

Tottenham Hotspur fan, quoted in
The Glory Game **by Hunter Davies**

"Of all the roles Chelsea are expected to fulfil - highest ticket prices in the league, snazziest restaurant, chairman with the most voluminous beard - winning the title is not one of them."

Jim White, writer and Manchester United fan in October 1998

"The worst crowd trouble I saw was down at Millwall. In the warm-up, there were people coming out of the crowd with meat-hooks in their heads. I think that's the only time I've been frightened in a game."

Chelsea's Ian Britton recalls a terrifying trip to The Den in 1976

"Even now when I'm asked for my autograph, I wonder if they were one of those who booed me."

Rangers' Ally McCoist remembers the bad times during his first stint with the club

"I've not renewed my season ticket,
because I'm not going to give the directors
my money. F*** them!"
West Ham fan and actor Ray Winstone

"Not so long ago, Boro were awful so I was
always cracking jokes about them. But since
they started doing well all my Boro gags
have gone down the tube. Bryan Robson
has a lot to answer for."
Comedian Roy 'Chubby' Brown

"It's good to be back at Wembley. We've been
here 12 times. That's more than Chelsea."
**Mick Jagger during The Rolling Stones
1996 world tour**

"I picked up an injury and spent quite a lot of time on the bench. One of the supporters knitted me a cushion to sit on, which said, 'Reserved for Brian Kilcline'."

The man known as "Killer" on home comforts at Newcastle United's St James' Park

"I believe the last man to score five times in a Chelsea shirt was David Mellor."

Tony Banks MP, July 1997, after Chelsea had put five past Manchester United

"Do I support a London football team? I do. I support Manchester United."

Model and geographer Caprice

"What I don't understand is how a Frenchman can be playing for Manchester United. He's not even from England."

Lord Denning QC comments on the Eric Cantona bust-up at Selhurst Park

"It was f****n' magic! When big Dunc Ferguson scored, I bloody exploded oot me seat, and so did Keegan!"

AC/DC singer Bryan Johnson recalls a visit to see his beloved Newcastle United

"I'm big on Aston Villa because the name is just so sweet. Other clubs are like 'Arrrrsenal' or 'Maaaan United' but Aston Villa sounds like a lovely spa."

Film star Tom Hanks

"What I don't understand is how a Frenchman can be playing for Manchester United. He's not even from England."

Lord Denning QC comments on the Eric Cantona bust-up at Selhurst Park

"Tony Banks described the English fans arrested in Marseille as brain-dead louts. This goes for me as well."

Labour MP Harriet Harman makes a slip

"If I go home and find Massimo Maccarone
in bed with my wife, I'm going to ask him
if he wants another blanket."
**Middlesbrough fan's reaction to the
Italian's miraculous late winner that gave
Middlesbrough a 4-3 aggregate UEFA Cup
semi-final victory over Steaua Bucharest
in April 2006**

"When the ball's down the Kop end, they
frighten the ball. Sometimes they suck
it into the back of the net."
Bill Shankly

"He's fat, he's round, he's sold your f**king ground, Al Fayed, Al Fayed..."

Various away fans at Fulham

"You had to be strong to be on the Kop. When I was about 13, I tried to go in the middle where all the excitement was and almost got cut in half. I was only 5 foot 7 inches. A big docker pushed the crowd back and I ducked out and went back to my usual place to the left of the goal."

Elvis Costello

"We hate Tuesday."

Millwall fans after Sheffield United fans chant "We hate Wednesday" at Bramall Lane

"Alvin, Alvin Martin, he's got no hair
but we don't care."

**West Ham fans chant for the popular
defender during the 1980s**

"Who let the frogs out, who? who? who? who?"

**Leicester City fans welcome Arsène
Wenger's Arsenal to the field**

"Rufus is a dog's name."

**Queen's Park Rangers fans to their
defender Rufus Brevett**

"You're Shish, and you know you are."

**Chelsea fans welcome Turkish side
Galatasaray to Stamford Bridge**

"It's just like watching Brazil."

Sung ironically by fans across the UK

"It's just like watching The Bill."

Blackburn Rovers fans respond to a

particularly large police cordon

"Joe Royle, Whatever you may do, You're

going down to Division Two. You won't

win a cup, You won't win a shield,

our next derby is Macclesfield."

Stockport County fans enjoy the

relegation of neighbour Manchester City

to the tune of 'Lord of the Dance'

"Niall Quinn's disco pants are the best,

They go up from his ar*e to his chest.

They're better than Adam and the Ants,

Niall Quinn's disco pants."

Manchester City fans celebrate their

striker's fashion sense

"You're just a small town in Burnley..."

Manchester City fans taunt Blackburn

Rovers supporters at Ewood Park

"Cannon and Ball are shagging your wife!"

Mancester City fans to Harry Kewell after

his wife appears on "I'm A Celebrity..."

"Do the social know you're here?"

London clubs to visiting northern teams

"Oh, Teddy, Teddy. You went to Man United
and you won f**k all."

**Arsenal fans rib the former Tottenham
Hotspur striker Teddy Sheringham after the
Gunners win the Double in 1998**

"I'm sure Arsenal fans are working on some
new chants, but they can sing what they like.
I've got three nice medals to show them."

**Teddy Sheringham looks forward to his
next match against Arsenal after winning
the Treble in 1999**

"Oh, Teddy, Teddy. You might have won
the Treble but you're still a c**t!"
Arsenal fans prove Teddy right

"We all agree, Jaap Stam is harder than Arnie!"
**Manchester United fans' chant at Sturm
Graz's Arnold Schwarzenegger Stadium
in December 2000**

"There's only one Carlton Palmer and
he smokes marijuana, He's 6 foot tall
and his head's too small, Livin' in a
Palmer wonderland!"
**Stockport County fans serenade
their manager, Carlton Palmer**

"We're supposed to be at home!"
Newcastle United fans singing in Barcelona
in December 2002, after torrential rain saw
their game postponed for 24 hours

"Come in a taxi, you must have come in a taxi.
Come in a taxi, you must have come in a taxi."
Birmingham City fans salute a sparse
Sunderland away contingent

"He's red, he's sound, he's banned from every
ground, Carra's dad, Carra's dad."
Liverpool fans honour Jamie Carragher's
dad, once arrested for being drunk
at a match

"I like watching matches, but I'm not certain about the scoring system."

Television presenter June Sarpong

"In my time players had short hair, wore long shorts and played in hob-nail boots. Now they have long hair, short shorts and play in slippers."

Arsenal's "Gentleman" Jack Crayston recalls different times

Chapter Eight: AWAY FROM THE PITCH

"At the end of the day, he scored three goals. Other than that, I kept him pretty quiet."

Reading's Michael Duberry had an easy afternoon against Fernando Torres

"I can't have a burger without putting on half a stone."

John Hartson worries about his weight

"I like the comfort of jeans and the elegance of a suit. But above all, I love the sensuality and sexuality that emanates from leather. It multiplies one's sensations tenfold."
Emmanuel Petit

"How can anyone say he's lazy? He is a sex symbol and has all that hair to blow-dry every day. That's an hour's job in itself."
Simon Mayo, Tottenham Hotspur fan and broadcaster, on David Ginola

"I prefer to frighten people by driving around in my white Porsche with Slipknot blaring out of the windows."
Reading goalkeeper Marcus Hahnemann

"I think I'd like to be in the fashion industry. I don't really know anything about it, but I reckon I'm great at choosing clothes. The things I buy are the best clothes in the world – or at least that's what I think."

Paul Parker

"Sometimes on a day off I go to the Krispy Kreme doughnut shop. When we play at home, I go there after the game and it's like a doughnut party! Everyone is eating doughnuts inside their cars – it's like a disco!"

Arsenal's Cesc Fabregas knows how to party

"The lifestyle is much the same – bad clothing, bad food – so we don't expect too much."

Alfie Haaland on why Norwegians settle so well in England

"When I see all my legs out, I have confidence. I look at my muscles and they look big and I feel strong. With big shorts, I can't see my muscles at all."

Paulo Di Canio on why he wore unfashionably short shorts

"I swear that when we first walked out on to the pitch most people thought we were the band!"

Robbie Fowler remembers the cream suits worn by Liverpool on FA Cup final day in 1996

"Barnesy's chucked me a couple of cast-offs, things he hasn't worn or he never really liked. A few years ago he gave me a jacket covered in the Chinese alphabet. I love it but it's a bit loud."
Barry Venison assessing Liverpool team-mate John Barnes' wardrobe

"José Mourinho sitting there smug and snug in his coat, the same one he's been wearing for twenty Januaries. Has he not heard of Oxfam?"
Hunter Davies, in the *New Statesman*, February 2005

"Is Chelsea's glory woven into José Mourinho's coat? Not since Joseph, the son of Jacob, has a coat acquired such symbolic significance."
Sarah Sands gets carried away in the *Daily Telegraph*, May 2005

"My hair is difficult, it's a problem! It doesn't always look healthy. But there's nothing I can do about it. If it was up to me I would have chosen a different kind of hair."
Every day's a bad hair day for Ricardo Carvalho

"I think I lost my barnet [hair] flicking the ball on for all them years at the near post from Brian Marwood's corners."
Arsenal's follicularly challenged Steve Bould

"At the end of the day, he scored three goals. Other than that, I kept him pretty quiet."
Reading's Michael Duberry had an easy afternoon against Fernando Torres

"I was full of it – I wanted to cuddle everyone I could see."
Jimmy Bullard can't keep his hands to himself after scoring

"When I looked down the leg was lying one way and my ankle was pointing towards Hong Kong – so I knew I was in serious trouble."
Manchester United's Alan Smith knows his geography

"In my time players had short hair, wore long shorts and played in hob-nail boots. Now they have long hair, short shorts and play in slippers."
Arsenal's "Gentleman" Jack Crayston recalls different times

"I think Pat's dress sense is dreadful. I would like to see him in a nice shirt or proper tie."
Mary Nevin, mother of former Chelsea winger Pat

"Luca wears some bad, bad underpants - like my grandfather wore. Big white underpants like they used 40 years ago."
Roberto Di Matteo on Gianluca Vialli

"I will be beautiful again in four or five days."

Cristiano Ronaldo reassures the female population after taking an elbow in the face

"I didn't see the ball. I just saw it going to my right."

Robert Green is selectively blind

"I sometimes put on my kids' Power Rangers outfits to chill out."

Trevor Sinclair likes to unwind

"Ed de Goey is the worst-dressed man I've ever seen. One pair of jeans, one pair of trainers, one shirt and one haircut."

John Terry on the Chelsea goalkeeper

"When I said I had no regrets I'd forgotten about that haircut and it has come back to haunt me on several occasions."
Former Everton and Rangers winger Trevor Steven on his permed mullet of the 1980s

"Never mix perms and drinking, it's a recipe for disaster."
Mick Lyons, former Everton captain

"My wife was a hairdresser and she decided to give me a new look. Nobody even recognized me when I went back and the commentators thought I was a new signing."
Everton's Paul Bracewell on his dramatic new barnet back in the 1980s

"No soup or pizza allowed inside for safety reasons."

Sign at away dressing room when Arsenal visited Man City after the 'Battle of the Buffet'

"At White Hart Lane, the two teams were going down the tunnel and I felt this tugging from behind. As I was about to step on to the pitch with 30,000 people watching, Gazza was trying to pull my shorts down. Luckily, they were tied firmly or I would have made my entrance with my kecks around my ankles."

David Seaman

"Arsenal are terrible. They can't even kick it over 50 yards. They have to pass it everywhere. It's a joke."

Reading's Marcus Hahnemann has his tongue firmly in his cheek

"I was going to cut my hair the other week and if I had done we'd have lost 1-0, so hooray for afros."

David James hails his expansive barnet

"Gary Kelly is the maddest one at Leeds United. Without prompting he was climbing headfirst into wheelie bins."

Paul Robinson remembers a Leeds United Christmas outing

"Being a robot, devoid of passion and spirit, is obviously the way forward for the modern-day footballer."
Gary Neville predicts the future

"My dad used to referee me when I was a kid. I remember him booking me – and asking my name."
Coventry's Kevin Kyle is a stranger to his own family

"I do it at home, as well, strolling around like Tarzan in just a pair of Nikes. The neighbours know me pretty well."
Gary Kelly on the fact he irons nude even when sharing a hotel room at away matches

"I was welcomed to Ibrox by McCoist
and Durrant spraying Ralgex all
over my underpants."
Iain Ferguson

"With Gazza around, you can expect to get
pepper in your dessert and it has been known
for him to book a sunbed for one of the black
players in the squad."
**Dennis Wise on England team-mate
Paul Gascoigne**

"The centre-forward's drunk, Mr Allison."
**Ted Drake to Arsenal manager George Allison
after he had just downed a bottle of lemonade
that was being used to highlight tactics**

"I only went in for a filling and I came out drunk - it must have been some anaesthetic! But get the video tapes of that tournament and you'll see how successful the dentist's chair was!"

Paul Gascoigne, recalling an infamous England squad drinking session prior to Euro 96

"We had a lot of laughs. The one thing which really sticks out was the day that Micky Fenton got a brand new Jaguar. He was really proud of it and we thought 'We'll fix him.' So the groundsman, Wilf Atkinson, and I got a pail of whitewash and painted it all over Micky's new car. Micky wasn't too pleased!"

Middlesbrough's Rolando Ugolini recalls the antics of the 1950s

"I don't really like the attention from girls – apart from anything else I already have a girlfriend. I like supporters of football whatever sex they are, but it's not so great when you're on a night out and girls just sit next to you ... but to be honest it doesn't happen to me that often anyway."

Gary Neville

"Liz Hurley, she's nice. I'd take her to Pizza Express – no posh restaurants. We'd go for a pizza then to watch Grease or something."

Phil Neville describes his ideal date back in 1996

"I had more different women than I scored goals. And I scored 23 goals."
Aston Villa's Gary Shaw on his prolific 1980-81 Championship-winning season

Headwaiter: "Mr Allison, your bar bill - I have to tell you, it is enormous."
Allison: "Is that all? You insult me. Don't come back until it's double that!"
Malcolm Allison

"I always said that a team who drinks together, wins together."
Richard Gough

"When I see Almunia's performances, I get angry and have to make a fist in my pocket."
Anger management, Jens Lehmann style

"It's weird having your name on a bag of crisps, but that's football."
Michael Owen sums up the essence of the beautiful game

"We're actually quite a tame bunch. I don't think a Tuesday night out once every six weeks is excessive."
Robbie Mustoe debunks the myth of Middlesbrough as a drinking club under Bryan Robson

"There used to be a drinking culture in football and I know because I was part of it."
John Aldridge

"The manager doesn't want me to live like a monk. If he tried to make me live like a monk my football would go down the drain. He understands that, we've had that conversation."
Dwight Yorke comes to an understanding with Sir Alex Ferguson

"We played like a bunch of drunks."
Yossi Benayoun hammers West Ham's performance

"I never socialized with Eric. My wife and I always said we would have him over, but we never got round to it. We always called round for the rent, but never to ask him over. That's terrible really, isn't it?"
Eric Cantona's former team-mate and landlord Mark Hughes

"It's disappointing to be dropped from any team – even my mates' fantasy league team."
Robert Green hates sitting on the bench

"If he stays out of nightclubs for the next few years, he can buy one."
Gérard Houllier predicting a glorious future for Steven Gerrard

"Everyone thought Brian was clean-living. You should have seen him crawling along the hotel corridor, drunk, while on pre-season tour."
John Brown reveals how Brian Laudrup was welcomed to Rangers

"I've only been to a pub once and that was to get cigarettes for my wife at 11.30 in the evening. I prefer bars to sit and drink tea or coffee."
José Mourinho gets into the swing of life in the UK

"Andrew Flintoff. He's the man of the moment. He's just a normal, good lad and the best cricketer in the world. And I chose him because he got absolutely rat-ar*ed on the parade!"

Chelsea's Frank Lampard, nominating his favourite non-footballing sportsman

"Modern-day newspapers would have had a field day just following Chelsea around. We wouldn't have been off the front or back pages."

David Webb on the 1970s side

"It was obvious from the moment we arrived in Baghdad and saw soldiers carrying machine guns that leisure activities would be limited."

Colin Pates on Chelsea's trip to Iraq, 1986

"McEwans Best Scotch!"

John Hendrie, when asked what made him come to Newcastle in 1988

"Toon army, Malcolm Macdonald, Kevin Keegan, John Hall and Julie's Nightclub!"

Pundit Andy Gray names five things Newcastle

"If we invite any player up to the quayside to see the girls and then up to our magnificent stadium, we will be able to persuade any player to sign."

Sir Bobby Robson on the myriad attractions of Tyneside

"Vaya ciudad – what a town!"

Columbian striker Tino Asprilla after his first

visit to Newcastle's famous Bigg Market

"We don't have reporters any more;

we have QCs. Nowadays they aren't

interested in how many goals a player

scores, but where he's scoring at night."

Everton manager Joe Royle in 1994

"If I could be a superhero, I would be Batman.

He's got the least silly tights."

Worryingly, Paul Robinson seems

to have thought this through...

"I know it was outside the box, but that should have been a penalty."
Robbie Savage needs to brush up on the laws of the game

"I hear Big Fergie likes a few pints, loves to stay out late and chase the birds and gives a bit of lip in training; in my book he has all the ingredients of a good footballer."
Jim Baxter, Rangers legend of the 1960s, on fellow Scot Duncan Ferguson

"Andy Gray is an ugly b*stard in the morning and I can vouch for that because I've slept with him a few times."
John Bailey recalls his Everton room-mate

"Every good team has a strong centre. I'd look round. Goalkeeper, Jim Cumbes. I'd think, 'What time did you get in last night?' Centre-half, Chris Nicholl. In the toilet putting his contact lenses in. Central midfield, Bruce Rioch. Shaking like a leaf. Centre-forward, Sammy Morgan. Next to Chris putting his contact lenses in. What chance did I have?"
Vic Crowe, Aston Villa manager of the early 1970s

"We were playing away and we'd taken this 15-year-old apprentice with us. As was the custom, a whisky bottle was passed round. Players took a drink, then when they'd gone on to the pitch Vic Crowe took a big swig. The apprentice asked him why and he replied, 'Son, when you're manager of this club you'll know why.'"

Jim Cumbes, Aston Villa goalkeeper in the early 1970s

"I think I was 5ft 9in at birth."

You've got to feel for Peter Crouch's mum

"It wasn't her wedding anniversary, it was her birthday, because there's no way I'd have got married in the football season. And it wasn't Rochdale. It was Rochdale Reserves."
Bill Shankly refuting stories that he had taken his wife Nessie to watch Rochdale on their wedding anniversary

"I dated a girl from Manchester and she showed me that steak pies and chips are very good."
Cristiano Ronaldo expands his culinary horizons

"A master of the art of love-making."
Former FA secretary Faria Alam on Sven-Göran Eriksson

"I do go to football sometimes but I
don't know the offside rule or free kicks –
or side kicks – or whatever they're called."
Victoria Beckham

"Who let the dogs out?"
**Victoria Beckham as Dwight Yorke's then
girlfriend Jordan takes her seat in the
players' enclosure at Old Trafford**

"God forbid if Alex Curran split up with
Steve Gerrard. Who would she be then?
You can't let a man make you."
**Singer Jamelia, boyfriend of
Millwall's Darren Byfield**

"It's because I'm engaged to one of the most famous footballers in the country. I can't help that. She'll be glad to know I don't know her boyfriend's name but Steven thinks he's lower than a non-league football player."

Alex Curran hits back

"We had a wonderful dinner. When we finished I was full of anticipation – but he wanted to clear the plates away first."

Faria Alam on Sven again

"I feel sorry for Nancy - not only does she look like a drag queen but she's latched on to someone who clearly doesn't love her."

Faria Alam on Sven's former partner Nancy Dell'Olio

"I can only believe what people say, he's frightened of her."

Sven conquest number two (that we know of) Ulrika Jonsson on Nancy Dell'Olio's hold over the unlikely lothario

"Well, it's only happened twice. That was it. But you see one betrays to launch a shout into the night."

Nancy Dell'Olio on Sven's infidelities

"I've already experienced worse moments in my life. It's a small problem, which needs time to be sorted out."

Ronaldo takes divorce in his stride

"He constantly wants sex because he thinks he can wear his groin out if it's being fixed. It's exhausting."

Harry Kewell's wife, Sheree Murphy, on hers husband's a pending groin operation

"I sorted out the team formation last night lying in bed with the wife. When your husband's as ugly as me, you'd only want to talk football in bed."

Harry Redknapp

"I don't have a thing for footballers."
Cristiano Ronaldo's on/off girlfriend Gemma Atkinson, formerly with Marcus Bent

"When you do bad things, he still wants to kill you, but that is a good thing for a manager."
Cristiano Ronaldo loves Alex Ferguson's mean streak

"If I have a lot of adrenaline in my body, that is helpful because I feel less pain."
Jens Lehmann is a big softie at heart

"When God was handing out brains Jonno decided to have a lie-in. He said to us recently 'There are two suns, aren't there? One here and one abroad.'"

Andrew Johnson reveals Jonathan Greening's Mensa credentials

"Sylvester Stallone isn't Rambo at home. And I'm not the person some people reckon I am."

David Bentley categorically denies being Rocky

"Sometimes it does happen – a child can fight with his father and they are still friends."

Emmanuel Adebayor reflects on his on-field spat with team-mate Nicklas Bendtner

"My team-mates call me 'The Thin Andy Fordham' but I'm a better darts player than him."
Robbie Savage fancies his chances on the oche

"I feel I can still do the same job as I did 10 years ago – I've just got a few more wrinkles."
David '100 caps' Beckham spends far too much time in front of the mirror

"Gary Neville is the club captain but has been injured for the best part of a year now and Giggsy's taken on the mantlepiece."
Rio Ferdinand reckons Ryan Giggs has been doing a spot of house clearing

"I don't need to demonstrate that I am the number one in the world. If I am named the best in the world, it won't be a surprise to me."
Cristiano Ronaldo is modesty itself

"That's the second time I've been sent off for celebrating. I'm going to staple my shirt on in future."
Sunderland winger Ross Wallace is prepared to take drastic measures to avoid a yellow card

"Why should I care if he goes elsewhere? We do not really talk."
Dave Kitson bids a fond farewell to Reading team-mate Steve Sidwell

"I've got a contract with United until 2010,
but my future belongs to God."
**Cristiano Ronaldo wants to play
for the Heaven XI**

"I have got big legs and a big backside
- it's just the way I am. I will always have
a big arse. I can't get rid of that."
**David Dunn rules out drastic
cosmetic surgery**

"I don't want to be modelling G-strings.
It's not that good for my image
- I'm a footballer not a tart."
Michael Owen, consummate professional

"Sometimes I dive, sometimes I stand. But I don't care about this. In football you can't stay up all the time."

Didier Drogba is a slave to gravity

"I like to sit around the house and watch TV programmes - but I really like playing football on my Xbox in my boxer shorts."

Cesc Fabregas, kinky gamer

"It was all that leek and potato soup I was brought up on in Wales."

Gary Speed reveals the secrets of his longevity

"The gaffer wanted me to kiss him but if my missus had seen me kissing him I would have been in trouble."
Crystal Palace's Clinton Morrison keeps his "other half" happy

"It augurs well that there are so many good young English keepers. Not that I care, I'm Scottish."
Watford's Malky Mackay on team-mate Ben Foster

"Wazza is in the groove. He is a spurter."
Rio Ferdinand on Wayne Rooney

"I can't have a burger without putting
on half a stone."

John Hartson worries about his weight

"I'm going to see a witch to see if she
can help me score."

Luis Boa Morte seeks magical intervention

"I was really surprised when the
FA knocked on my doorbell."

Michael Owen. Well, who wouldn't be?

"For as long as you're out injured, it takes
twice as long to get back. So I'm looking
to be back when I'm about 38."

Harry Kewell is planning a long career

"Not being involved on match days was unbearable, especially the last four games I played in."
James McFadden can't remember when he was on the bench or not

"When you see Damien [Duff] coming out of the shower, you'd never believe he's a professional footballer."
What exactly is Didier Drogba trying to say?

"I hate to admit this but I don't even know how to make a cup of tea or coffee. I can boil a kettle for a pot noodle and I've been known to warm up some food in the microwave."

Michael Owen really needs looking after

"I'm about as fast as me Nana!"

Robbie Fowler isn't as fast as he used to be

"Everything in England is shut at 5pm, there is nothing to do, nowhere to go. I just got bored."

Jose Antonio Reyes does his bit for the English Tourist Board...

"We have such terrible weather that often there is nothing to do but watch football and drink beer."

...As does Reading's Dave Kitson

"If this does not change quickly, I will have to go to a witch doctor because there is some kind of wizardry as to why I have not scored."

Carlos Tevez just cannot understand his goal drought

"I'm the kind of player who trains well every day. Do I sound like the teacher's pet?"

Yes, Jamie Carragher, you do

"I got hit in the nose again – and with the size of my nose I'm surprised they didn't have to evacuate the Riverside."

Robbie Savage is a right bleeder

"Lampard is a specialist in insulting people very badly."

Jens Lehmann doesn't rate Frank Lampard's swearing prowess

"He's like a second wife."

Benni McCarthy on his special relationship with Jason Roberts

"In football, I don't like to lose."

Andrei Shevchenko has a simple philosophy

"London is the best city in the world. It's a sea port where hundreds of languages are spoken and where football is played."
Michael Essien fancies a job with the London Tourist Board

"I couldn't tell you what is wrong with my feet but I've just never liked them."
Claudio Pizarro is no foot fetishist

"Goalkeeping is like extreme sports sometimes – you have to let yourself go."
Jens Lehmann on the custodian's art

"I'll take any goal, any time, any place, anywhere - you can call me the Martini striker."

Carlton Cole, cocktail comedian

"Phil Neville once scored against me and, oh my gosh, it was the worst day of my life."

David James is still having nightmares

"Quite simply, it is true that I can be a pig! It is not a lie to say that. Sometimes, I feel I am in the right even when I'm in the wrong."

Thierry Henry reveals his mean streak

"I don't enjoy games much. I'm not a skilful player who can have much fun on the pitch."

Javier Mascherano is a miseryguts

"I don't know why he's called me an elephant seal... except for my changing-room party trick where I shuffle along on my stomach and catch fish from the other players."

Trevor Benjamin loves to entertain

"Al Pacino is my favourite actor and I always take my copy of The Godfather trilogy with me. I often put one on safe in the knowledge that if I drop off, it doesn't really matter because I already know the ending."

Kevin Nolan, film buff

"It will be a difficult couple of days. It's difficult now and it will be difficult tomorrow."

Gary Neville predicts a difficult 48 hours

"At the moment I'm just swallowing it all as part of the humiliation but I think – and this is aimed at my dear manager – one shouldn't humiliate players for too long."

Jens Lehmann is fed up with Arsene Wenger

"Tony Blair was on Football Focus the other week and named me as one of his favourite players. My father-in-law phoned me and said 'I've never heard such rubbish!' I voted Lib-Dem last time but I'm Labour again now."

The PM gets Arjan De Zeeuw's vote

"It is like an addiction, like a drug, you just want more and more of it."

Brett Emerton just loves scoring

"I was fishing and there were some six-year-olds peppering me with songs on the other side of the bank. I trod on my pole and went straight into the water. I crawled out but I had weeds in my hair."
Jimmy Bullard does his 'Creature From The Black Lagoon' impression

"I always had the belief that if you put five men in front of me, I could go past them all."
Cristiano Ronaldo doesn't suffer from modesty

"I like the money, but of course teachers should get more than us. I'm not saying footballers should save the environment and change the NHS, but if we portrayed ourselves 15 per cent better then it would help."

Brad Friedel thinks players need to think about their image

"I'm a big fan of heavy rock music like AC/DC but the lads never let me play it in the dressing room as it's too loud. I love the rock lifestyle and as a kid it was my main ambition to be a rock star. Hopefully I've got the next best thing."

David Bentley reveals his musical frustrations

"Taricco fell over and his feet were in the air. He pushed them out and hit me in the chest on purpose and, as some foreigners do, he was rolling around like a little girl."

Glen Johnson endears himself to the Premiership's imports

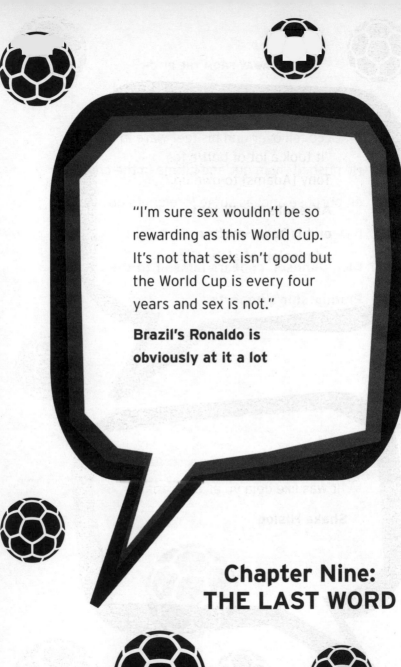

"I'm sure sex wouldn't be so rewarding as this World Cup. It's not that sex isn't good but the World Cup is every four years and sex is not."

Brazil's Ronaldo is obviously at it a lot

Chapter Nine:
THE LAST WORD

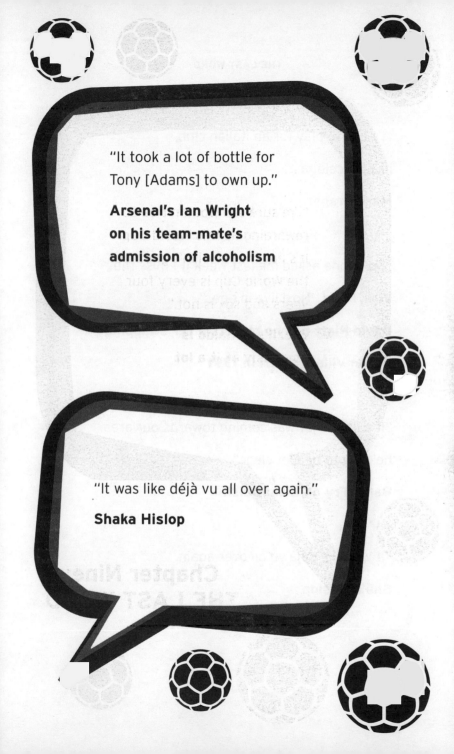

"It took a lot of bottle for Tony [Adams] to own up."

Arsenal's Ian Wright on his team-mate's admission of alcoholism

"It was like déjà vu all over again."

Shaka Hislop

"I'd like to play for an Italian club, like Barcelona..."
Mark Draper

"Someone asked me last week if I miss the Villa. I said, 'No, I live in one.'"
David Platt has no regrets after swapping Aston Villa for Bari in 1991

"If a jumbo jet was coming towards our area, he'd try to head it clear."
Barry Fry on Liam Daish

"It was like déjà vu all over again."
Shaka Hislop

"It's not nice going to the supermarket and the woman at the till thinking, 'Dodgy keeper'."

David James on his loss of form in 1997

"It's a good advert for the cricket season."

Mark Lawrenson isn't impressed by the FA Cup final

"I've never had a good record in the FA Cup – apart from winning it."

Gary McAllister is his own harshest critic

"I'm sure sex wouldn't be so rewarding as this World Cup. It's not that sex isn't good but the World Cup is every four years and sex is not."

Brazil's Ronaldo is obviously at it a lot

"The lads used to call me 'the Judge' because I sat on the bench so much."
Les Sealey

"It took a lot of bottle for Tony [Adams] to own up."
Arsenal's Ian Wright on his team-mate's admission of alcoholism

"I have a good record there. Played one, won one, and hopefully it will be the same after Saturday."
Steven Gerrard crosses his fingers

"Goalkeepers aren't born today until they're in their late twenties or thirties."

Kevin Keegan offers an explanation

"It wasn't my choice to become a goalkeeper, but I was probably too violent to play outfield."

Peter Schmeichel

"Djimi Traore had to adapt to the English game and he did that by going out on loan to Lens last season."

Ian Rush on Djimi Traore

"I'm not superstitious, but every
time she comes we lose"
**Steve Coppell wishes his mother would
stay away from the Madejski Stadium**

"Matches don't come any bigger than
FA Cup quarter-finals."
Neil Warnock

"Even when they had Moore, Hurst and
Peters, West Ham's average finish was
about 17th, which just shows how cr*p the
other eight of us were."
Harry Redknapp

"With the foreign players it's more difficult. Most of them don't even bother with the golf, they don't want to go racing. They don't even drink"

'Arry again

"Dani is so good-looking I don't know whether to play him or f*ck him"

...and again

"I started clapping myself, until I realized that I was Sunderland's manager."

Peter Reid after Dennis Bergkamp

scores for Arsenal

"He's a fantastic player. When he isn't drunk."
Brian Laudrup on Paul Gascoigne

"Footballers are only interested in drinking,
clothes and the size of their willies."
Karren Brady

"In 1969 I gave up women and alcohol. It was
the worst 20 minutes of my life."
George Best

"He uttered the six worst words in the English
language: 'I want to play for Liverpool.'"
Everton's Bill Kenwright on Nick
Barmby after his switch of allegiance
following Euro 2000

"I don't think there's anyone bigger or smaller than Maradona."

Kevin Keegan

"There was plenty of fellers who would kick your bollocks off."

Nat Lofthouse

The unthinkable is not something we are thinking about at the moment."

Then Manchester United chief executive Peter Kenyon

"It was handcuffs at dawn"

Sir Alex Ferguson mixes his metaphors

"To be marooned on a desert island with an endless supply of lager, women and Sky TV."
Ian Walker describes his chief ambition

"Roy Keane is Damien, the devil incarnate off the film The Omen. He's evil. Even in training."
Ryan Giggs

"I rang my secretary and said, 'What time do we kick off tonight?' and she said, 'Every ten minutes.'"
Alan Ball during his troubled year as Manchester City manager in 1996

"Celtic manager Davie Hay still has a fresh pair of legs up his sleeve."

John Greig

"There's as much chance of McAvennie leaving as there is of us losing 5-1 tomorrow."

Billy McNeill, Celtic manager, on 26 August 1988. Celtic lost 5-1 to Rangers at Ibrox the following day. Frank McAvennie was subsequently transferred to West Ham

"I wouldn't put my house on it. I've worked too hard over 35 years to get a house."

Gordon Strachan isn't exactly brimming with confidence ahead of Celtic's Champions League showdown with Barcelona

"It doesn't matter what happened in the game – we got the three points."
Wayne Bridge fails to grasp the concept of the Carling Cup final

"Once Tony Daley opens his legs, you're in trouble."
Howard Wilkinson

"I couldn't settle in Italy – it was like living in a foreign country."
Ian Rush

"I'm not going to look beyond the semi-final – but I would love to lead Newcastle out at the final."
Sir Bobby Robson

"I prefer it in Newcastle, knowing all the people want me here. They look me in the eye and say, 'I want to play with you.'"
David Ginola

"I remember Jimmy Adamson crowing after Burnley had beaten us that his players were in a different league. At the end of the season they were."
Bob Paisley

"And they were lucky to get none."
Newcastle United legend Len Shackleton after the 13-0 defeat of Newport County in 1946

"Where are we in relation to Europe?

Not far from Dover"

Harry Redknapp

"My father had five sons. I had four brothers"

Sir Bobby again

"I can't promise anything, but I promise

100 per cent."

Paul Power

"He arrived like a giraffe on roller skates."

**Rob McCaffrey's bizarre description of Niall
Quinn's equalizer in his debut for Manchester
City against Chelsea in 1990**

"Juan is something special. Manchester United have bought a true great. There are few players in the world who you can say possess everything. But, yes, Juan Verón is one of those few. I believe he will one day be remembered as a true great of our game. United have got a player who can follow in the footsteps of all the legendary players they have had at the club."

Diego Maradona speaks too soon

Aye, Everton."

Bill Shankly to a barber who asked him if he wanted anything off the top

"If you're in the penalty area and don't know what to do with the ball, put it in the net and we'll discuss the options later."
Bob Paisley

"I daren't play in a five-a-side at Liverpool, because if I collapsed, no one would give me the kiss of life!"
Graeme Souness as his popularity waned

"The Champions League? I won it with Liverpool and now I want to win it with Juventus."
Momo Sissoko experienced a memory lapse, having joined Liverpool two months after their 2005 triumph.

"My reputation will always precede me to the day I die. For some people, that probably can't be quickly enough."
Controversial Newcastle midfielder Joey Barton gave an honest assessment of himself.

"He sat downstairs as if it was the most normal thing for a multi-millionaire footballer to do."
A passenger who spotted Man City striker Robinho and his girlfriend on a bus to the shopping centre.

"He rang me before he got on the plane to tell me he didn't have a key, so I waited up for him." **Theo Walcott's mother waiting for the England hat-trick hero to return from Croatia.**

Gareth Jellyman of Mansfield Town has been sent off, hope he doesn't throw a wobbly!" **Jeff Stelling**

"Ghana are finding it difficult to impregnate the Cameroon defence." **Eurosport commentator**

"Last year's race was a bit of a damp squid." **Mark Hateley**

"It's never over until it's over, but this is over."

Chris Kamara

"I've got more points on my licence!"

Derby manager Paul Jewell on his side's

meagre points total.

"Their goals were just comedy. You'd
probably win £250 on Candid Camera
for that second one."

Crystal Palace boss Neil Warnock

You can't beat Sinatra. I was actually supposed
to have dinner with him one night, but we lost
to Charlton so I cancelled it and went home!"

Sir Alex Ferguson

"The reception I got at Upton Park wasn't too bad considering I now manage one of their biggest rivals. Mind you, it helped that I didn't get out of my seat for 90 minutes."

Redknapp on returning to West Ham.

It's no coincidence that the three teams that have been relegated are the ones that have conceded the most goals.

Manchester City boss Joe Royle

I am glad that David Beckham will be fit. Now England will have no excuses when we beat them.

Germany's Sebastian Deisler before England's 5-1 victory in Munich

I've got a little bit of a headache, that's how nerve-wracking it was, but I've enjoyed the whole night.

David Beckham

I must admit I have a dressing room curiosity over Beckham. I want to see if he is equipped as he is in the underwear adverts."

AC Milan striker Marco Borriello

"I will bust a gut to play in any game."

Michael Owen on rapid recovering from stomach surgery.

"I think there might be one or two games
where I don't get some decisions going for me
- from people who have read my book!"
**Warnock fears his honest autobiography
might have been a little too honest**

"That was more by luck than good fortune."
Paul Parker

"I can see the carrot at the end of the tunnel."
Stuart Pearce